FOUR PORTALS TO POWER

FOUR PORTALS TO POWER

A PRACTICAL GUIDE TO TRUE SELF-MASTERY FOR LEADERS

••••

DEAN HERMAN, Ph.D.

EURUS PRESS

San Francisco

Although anyone may find the insights, approaches, and tools in this book to be useful, it is made available with the understanding that neither the author nor the publisher is engaged in presenting specific medical, psychological, or emotional advice. Nor is anything in this book intended to be a diagnosis, prescription, recommendation, or cure for any medical, psychological, or emotional condition. Each person has unique needs and this book cannot take these individual differences into account. Each person should engage in a program of treatment, prevention, cure, or general health only in consultation with a licensed, qualified physician, therapist, or other competent professional.

Eurus Press
555 California Street, Suite 300
San Francisco, CA 94104
Telephone: 415-296-0220
Email: info@EurusPress.com

Quantity sales: Special discounts are available on quantity purchases by corporations, associations, and others. For details, contact the publisher.

Printed in the United States of America

Eurus Press books are printed on long-lasting acid-free paper. The paper in this book is 30% post-consumer waste.

Library of Congress Control Number: 2010926499

ISBN 978-0-9845452-0-9

15 14 13 12 11 10   10 9 8 7 6 5 4 3 2

To Nava Shira ("Beautiful Song")
and
Simcha Lev ("Happy Heart")

CONTENTS

INTRODUCTION

What we achieve inwardly will change outer reality.
—PLUTARCH

This book is a guide to assist you in becoming more truly powerful—as a person and as a leader. You may be a leader within an organization, an institution, a community, or even a family. At the very least, you are the leader of your own life. If you view yourself as a leader in any of these different forms and you want more power—the type of power that comes from *within*—this book is for you.

True power is not the ability to exercise force. Nor is it the ability to acquire by manipulation. As you will see, these are forms of illusory power. True power is simply the ability, originating from *inside* the person, to make things happen. It requires you to master yourself and your inherent capacities, which I will explain to you. This book is a road map for achieving that self-mastery. If you study and apply the lessons here, you will be far more powerful as a person and as a leader than you thought was possible.

So this book is for you if you have a nagging sense that you really could be doing more in your life or in your leadership—*and* you suspect what's holding you back is something inside of you. Read on if, instead of looking outward to blame, you are prepared to look inward to have greater impact.

This book is also for you if you are repeatedly coming up against the same obstacles—and you are willing to consider that the obstacles are more internal than external. This may sound like you asking, "How come I just can't seem to _____?" Fill in the blank with any limitation you continuously encounter.

The potential obstacles are nearly endless. Yours might be, "How come I just can't seem to get the people I lead to be as energized and committed as I am?" Or ". . . get myself to be more consistently positive?" Or "more confident?" Or "less irritable?" Or "more passionate?" Your challenge might also be in your personal life—as in, for example, "Why can't I get my spouse (or children or people in general) to respond more positively to me?"

It's common for people to be tormented by these kinds of gaps in their personal and leadership power. Sometimes they give up and say to themselves, "I guess I just can't do it." Or they say, "That's just my personality." But you need not succumb and accept personal defeat. With this book, you can transcend your seeming limitations and be consistently more powerful. I will show you how.

Many leaders, though, are misguided in their efforts to grow more powerful. Whether they are business leaders, nonprofit leaders, or the leaders of our communities or even nations, the actions they take often undermine their own power. And so we can observe many struggling and unsuccessful leaders. This is all unnecessary. It stems from the failure to understand power and how to enhance it.

The guidance here grows out of my own experience and evolution as a psychologist and executive consultant. As I consulted to and trained thousands of leaders around the world—in North America, Europe, Asia, and Australia—I soon came to see that something more was required than focusing on the leader's behavior. Many executives I worked with had already used coaches. They had already received many behavioral prescriptions. So they knew some of what they should be doing differently. Yet they continued doing the same things and bumping up against the same limitations. For the great majority of them, their performance was already strong overall. But they wanted more for themselves. And I wanted to help them.

I concluded that I needed to work at deeper levels, identifying and addressing the *root causes* of their limitations. And I also concluded that I would need to work with the whole person, including his passion, his emotions, and his inspiration.

The result of this challenge was my development of a comprehensive system for understanding and enhancing human power. This system of *four powers* provides specific guidance for mastering the four core human powers—or capacities—of emotion, passion, intellect, and inspiration. As I worked with my clients globally, I continuously tested and refined the system to make it as broadly useful and potent as possible.

The system is now at a point where it is an elegant and powerful structure that leaders use to transform themselves—and that I use to aid them in that process. And I continue to work on improving the system. I expect I will never be finished developing it because that would mean I have "finished" my own self-development as a consultant.

It is this system of four powers that I will illustrate here for you. The system is *comprehensive*. Nearly every leadership challenge can be mastered by diligent and thoughtful application of the principles set forth in this book. The system is also *logical*. Therefore, it is easy to understand and all its components smoothly integrate together.

And the system is *powerful*. By applying it, you will soon see for yourself visible and substantial results. As I personally draw on the system moment by moment to offer leaders insights about themselves and tools for change, I notice them gaining a truly enhanced capacity. Ultimately, the underlying formula is simple: Deep and profound insights lead to deep and profound change.

When I started working in these deep ways with my clients, I was not quite sure how my approach would be received. I found to my delight that it was typically very much welcomed. Executives recognize,

I've learned, that just as they need a deeper understanding of their businesses, products, and services to be most successful, so, too, do they need a deeper understanding of themselves in order to achieve greater personal success.

I am honored that so many invited me to work with them in these ways. And I am humbled by the transformative effect that my work has had for them. The system I am about to share with you was a gift given to me. And so now I want to—and need to—share it with you.

My inspiration in writing this book was heightened by a belief that is central for me. I believe that when people, and especially leaders, progress in their self-awareness and self-mastery, the results go beyond their just becoming more effective. They also make the world a better place in which to live. I myself have far to go in expanding my own self-awareness and self-mastery. So I continuously work on those areas to become a better leader and a better human being. I am thrilled to help others on that quest as well. It is my hope that in reading this book, you and those you lead will enjoy greater success, and also greater well-being.

The stories and examples in this book are drawn from my consulting experiences with many leaders. In order to protect their privacy, I have changed a number of the facts so that no individual clients will be identifiable. And although the stories are mostly about leaders, they are also very much about human beings just like you and me. In fact, if we bear in mind that we are all the leaders of our own lives, then this book applies to every one of us in all aspects of our daily living.

Looking back over many years, I remember a number of the leaders I've served asking me to write this book. They told me how valuable and transformative our work together had been. They wanted a book that they and others could continuously use and refer to.

Yet I took much time before finally deciding to write this book. I was concerned whether I could capture the beauty and the magic that unfolds between myself and my clients. And I was concerned that it might be too much for those not prepared to step into a larger realm of power. I have since put those concerns to rest. I trust that this book will find its way to those who are ready for a powerful transformation in how they live and in how they lead.

A NOTE ON HOW TO READ THIS BOOK

I have intentionally written this book in a way that is compact and condensed. My aim was to make each section of each chapter sufficiently rich in content that it would mobilize and support deep change within you. Therefore, I do not recommend that you read large portions of the book in single sittings, as you would likely take in far more than you could fully absorb.

So instead, read no more than a chapter at a time. Sometimes, you might even want to read no more than a section of a chapter. And after every section, put the book down for at least a moment and reflect. Ask yourself, "How can I apply what I've learned?" Or, "What will I start doing differently today?"

Some changes you will be able to make immediately. Other, deeper change may require more time. Overall, let the profound shifts this book maps out unfold within you over the period that is right for you. And let this book continuously guide you throughout that process as you grow increasingly wise—and increasingly powerful.

Let us now begin our journey.

1

INTEGRATE THE PRINCIPLES OF POWER INTO YOUR LIFE AND YOUR LEADERSHIP

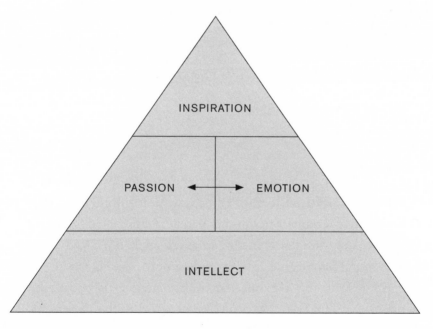

The Four Powers Pyramid

LOOK AT YOURSELF AND PREPARE
TO MAGNIFY YOUR POWER

Your greatest power is inside of you. It includes your capacity to master yourself and master the impact you have on other people. Because this power is entirely internal, you have complete control over it and you can enhance it dramatically. Yet, if you are like most leaders, you neglect to do so. Once you clearly see how much that harms you and those around you, you will be more energized to magnify this power that is so fundamental to you.

Have you ever worked with a colleague, or even a boss, who acted in ways that seemed ineffective to you? Perhaps he didn't quite know how to evoke positive responses from other people. Perhaps you found her to be too weak or too aggressive. Or perhaps he could not control his own emotions and his energy levels. Regardless of the details, you may have said to yourself with some concern and exasperation, "Why does she act in these ways?" Or even, "Why do I have to work with this person?"

One late Friday afternoon in winter, I met a struggling CEO for our first meeting. As you read about him, ask yourself, "Have I known similar leaders?" As the last rays of the setting sun streamed through the window, he leaned back in his swivel chair and spoke of how he had built his company "from a one-man shop into a $400 million-a-year enterprise." Yet, he confided, his executives were currently showing "a lack of passion." In the previous six weeks, in fact, he had lost three of them. The first he had fired, and the other two had quit. "I think," he surmised, "I've been making bad hiring decisions."

I learned a different perspective when I interviewed the remaining members of his team. They were open with me because they knew that although I'd quote them, I would not reveal who had made which comments. Most of the executives described their boss as "critical," "irritable," or "testy." Some of them were resentful, while others were intimidated and anxious. The overall feeling of the team was summarized by one executive in his 50s: "I just don't trust him," he said. "I don't trust him to show up in a way that is unemotional, fair, and respectful."

When I presented my written findings to the CEO, complete with many such direct quotes, his demeanor changed. He looked up at me from reading the report and quietly said, "I created all of this, didn't I?" Up until that point, he had failed to recognize how much his emotions were driving his actions. And he had failed to recognize that just like him, his people had become afraid, resentful, and unsure of their own value—and that he was the cause of this very outcome.

This CEO had not understood the root causes of his business problems. He had not understood that those causes were inside of him—and that, therefore, he had more control over them than anything else. He had not understood the true nature of his power. You may know of such leaders. They mean well. But they are destroying their companies.

As was true for this CEO, your greatest power is inside of you. It is within your personality. It is in your emotions and how you manage them. It is in how you manage your thoughts as well. And it is in your passion and your inspiration. Because all this power is within you, it is under your control. It is truly *your* power, and you can enhance it dramatically. Or you can let it shrivel. In this book, I will show you how to access and develop this power so that you can be a far more impactful leader.

But before we go forward, it is necessary that you first look at yourself and consider some difficult questions. Consider whether, in some ways, you may be just like the CEO you read about. He was helplessly pulling the wrong levers as his ship was sinking. Are you doing the same thing? In at least one aspect of your leadership? Or in at least one part of your life?

Notice where you are falling short of where you want to be. What isn't working for you? Are you ready to stop looking only outward for explanations and ready to start looking inward?

If you need examples, look at your colleagues, family members, and friends. You can probably see how each of them has gaps in self-awareness and self-mastery. If you look closely, you can likely see how those gaps hurt them and even other people. Do you think you don't have such gaps, too? So take back your power by looking inside. Train the spotlight on yourself steadfastly—and with compassion. What gaps do you see and what harm are they causing?

For instance, where has your self-doubt held you back from seizing opportunities? Where have your resentments weakened and ruptured your relationships? Where have your fears shrunk your range of options? Are you always alive with passion? Notice where you are stuck and blocked. Notice the extent to which you are truly inspired. And the extent to which you are not. Each of these areas and more present opportunities to you to be more powerful.

So take a moment and reflect, "What have I been wanting to make happen but have so far been unable to do?" Consider both your work life and your personal life, too. How much longer do you want these frustrations to continue? Likely, most of them are really not necessary. You have far greater power than you realize. Much of it is now dormant, awaiting your efforts to access it and develop it. In the pages that follow, I will show you how to do so.

KEY POINTS TO REMEMBER

- It is your internal power, more than anything else, that determines your success in work and in life. This power includes your capacity to manage your emotions, thoughts, passion, and inspiration.

- As this power is within you, it is completely under your control and you can enhance it greatly.

- To the extent you have not developed your internal power and fall short of self-mastery, you are needlessly harming yourself and those around you.

- You will enjoy an enhanced ability to create the results important to you when you turn your focus inward and attend to developing your power. This book will provide you clear maps and instructions for doing so.

ACTIONS TO ENHANCE YOUR POWER

- As you start your journey into this book to grow your power, take an inventory of where you are now. This will help focus your reading and your efforts to magnify your power.

  - For the first part of your inventory, make a list of where you lack self-mastery. For example, you may lack full self-confidence in certain contexts. Or despite your efforts not to, you may often be irritable with certain people. Include all areas where your lack of mastery of your emotions, your energy levels, and your impact on other people is limiting you. To heighten your motivation for addressing these areas, consider writing, next to each item on your list, the specific harm it causes you and/or others.

  - For the second part of your inventory, answer the question, "What do I want to make happen but have so far been unable to do?" Let your list include items from both your work life and your personal life.

  - As you read this book, refer back to the two lists you have just made so that you can create change and enhance your power in the ways that are most meaningful for you.

KNOW THE FOUR POWERS INSIDE OF YOU
TO HEIGHTEN YOUR IMPACT

The power within you consists of four distinct and complementary capacities: the powers of intellect, passion, emotion, and inspiration. They are ordered hierarchically in the Four Powers Pyramid. That pyramid provides a map of their development within you. As you master the four powers, you will increasingly be able to create results that benefit you and those you serve. It is this mastery that will largely determine your success as a leader.

Your power actually consists of four different and complementary capacities. Think of them as four potent allies always there to serve you. And as you feed and develop them, they will grow ever stronger. These four capacities are displayed in the Four Powers Pyramid on page 7. Their hierarchical arrangement shows the degree of assistance they can provide you. Their positions within the pyramid also show the usual sequence of their development.

I will guide you in mastering these four powers, step by step. As you gain that mastery, you will experience an ever-increasing capacity to make things happen. And this is all that power really is—the ability to create results. You will also discover an increasing ease and solidity in your leadership and in your daily living. Then you will be less easily knocked off balance by the many stresses and obstacles that you, as a leader, are likely to encounter. In later chapters, I will describe in detail how you can master each of the four powers. For now, I will take you through a brief introduction to each of them.

Let's start with the power of intellect. Its position at the bottom of the pyramid doesn't mean that it is unimportant. Actually, this power is essential for you. It is the capacity to reason, the ability to effectively use logic. It is more than intellectual ability, which I've found is rarely an issue among leaders. It is also the use of that ability to communicate and to influence in ways that create greater impact. Many people, particularly in business, are so trained in analyzing issues logically that they will not trust your ideas unless you provide a logical rationale for them. To be taken seriously, you will often need to open with logic.

But your logic, your power of intellect, is not enough. It opens the door for you. It is the first step in gaining people's attention and support. But more is needed. People aren't so moved by your logical arguments. When they hear them, they may nod and they may agree in their minds. But typically, they will not be moved to take action. For that to happen, you need to use at least one of the other powers at your disposal. You need to impassion the people you speak with, inspire them, or create positive emotions in them that will impel them into action.

Yet many leaders fail to do any of this. They default to using the power of their intellect almost exclusively. And that greatly limits their effect on other people. How about you? As you read about the other three powers, ask yourself, "To what extent am I using them? To what extent am I overly depending on my intellect to stir people into action?"

"I used to have the most elaborate and logical rationales for my ideas," a vice president of engineering once told me. "Actually, I thought many of my proposals were brilliant. So if people didn't agree with me and

When you speak with your colleagues, you may believe it is important to show your careful and thoughtful analyses in support of your points. But most likely, they are not following you. Few people are inclined to listen to a logical argument for very long. They get bored or distracted. Or they just can't "keep up" and may feel intellectually overwhelmed. By using your other three powers, you can more fully engage with your colleagues and be a more impactful leader.

support me, I'd think they were just idiots. After a while, because I was getting so little buy-in, I thought everyone was an idiot—except for me, of course. As you can guess, I wasn't very effective."

My client had come to realize that the power of his intellect was not enough. Logic only causes people to think. What he needed was people to take action—action that would support him. This required him to learn about and use his three other powers, each of which is a potent capacity inside of you.

At the next level of the pyramid are two powers side by side. These two powers, passion and emotion, work in tandem. Passion is your life energy; it resides within your body. When we say a leader is passionate, we mean that she shows a lot of energy. When a CEO says, "I need the employees to be more engaged," he's saying, in effect, "I need them to show more passion." As you will see later in this book, a leader's passion activates other people's passion. Therefore, this is a crucial power for you to develop as a leader.

POWER OF PASSION
Life energy that is demonstrated through words and actions.

Sometimes leaders come to me and say, "Dean, I need to be more passionate. Help me increase my passion." I tell them there are things they can do to directly accomplish that goal. But typically, the most important task for these leaders is not so much *increasing* their passion, but *unblocking* the passion that is already there.

For example, one of my clients came across as particularly bland. Although he was exceptionally astute in planning major business acquisitions, his energy was so subdued that you might barely notice him in a room with other people. He complained to me that he'd been told he needed to be more passionate. Yet he had no idea how to accomplish that objective. He protested, "I can't change my personality."

Yet, we found in our work together that he actually had a strong inner fire of passion—with many fears and much self-doubt covering it up. We saw, for example, that he spoke in such flat and constricted tones at meetings because he wanted to avoid a lot of attention. As one of his colleagues put it, he preferred "hiding behind a cloud of words." And we found that he would express each of his ideas so deliberately and carefully—in a way that was boring for others—because he was fearful of misstating a fact or a line of reasoning. This leader's passion did not need to be increased. It was already there, ready to shine once we worked together to remove its blockages.

As was true with this client, it is negative emotions that block passion. It is emotions such as fear, anger, and feelings of inadequacy. Can you recognize the presence of these emotions within you too? Naturally, they arise within nearly all people. To the extent you experience them, they will hinder the free flow of your energy.

Your challenge, then, is to transform these negative emotions into positive ones. When you do so, your passion will be unblocked. And it will be expressed through positive feelings such as excitement, enthusiasm, and joy. This is why the Four Powers Pyramid shows a double arrow between passion and emotion. These powers work in tandem.

None of this will be surprising as you reflect on your own experiences. Can you feel passionate—in any part of your life—when you are feeling anxious? Or angry? Or full of self-doubt? You must change these negative emotions and indeed transform them before your passion can be released.

The power of emotion, therefore, is of utmost importance to you. It determines whether your passion—and the passion of those who look to you and who are led by you—will be obstructed or will surge forth. So it is essential that you develop this power within you.

With this power, you can be aware of and transform your own emotions. And as you enhance that capacity, you will grow a parallel ability

definition

POWER OF EMOTION
The capacity to be aware of and transform your own emotions. This typically engenders the parallel capacity to be aware of and transform other people's emotions.

to be aware of and transform other people's emotions as well. So you will know what you are feeling and what others are feeling, too. And then you will adeptly transform any negative feelings into positive ones. Imagine how powerfully you could move and energize people through the use of these abilities. I will help you develop them in the pages that follow.

The final power, at the top of the pyramid, is the power of inspiration. To inspire means to bring *in spirit*. Spirit is not necessarily a spiritual entity. Rather, it is simply the unifying force among people. It is something bigger than any one of us. And it connects us all with each other.

Depending on your beliefs, you may experience spirit as a religious

definition

POWER OF INSPIRATION
The capacity to bring *spirit in*. Spirit is the unifying force among people. It provides people an experience of being part of something greater than their separate selves. One example is "team spirit."

or spiritual presence. You may experience it in the sense of "team spirit" or "company spirit." You may feel it, therefore, in a church or a temple. You may also feel it at an athletic contest as you cheer for "your team." And you may feel it when an inspirational leader speaks to you and your colleagues about how you, as a team or as an organization, can join together to accomplish something meaningful that you could not do alone. You will be inspired to the extent you are lifted out of yourself and find an identity in something larger than who you normally believe yourself to be.

We human beings naturally hunger to be part of a greater whole beyond our limited, separate selves. The inspirational leader who provides her people that experience and harnesses the synergies that result will therefore be extraordinarily impactful and powerful. The power of inspiration is thus at the highest level in the pyramid.

The position of this power in the pyramid also signifies that the other powers, and especially the power of emotion, must be sufficiently

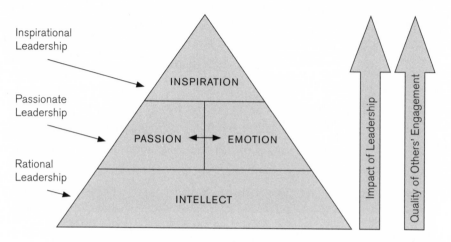

FIGURE 1.1 Impact of the Four Powers

developed first. As you will see as you read further, until you are solid and stable in how you manage your emotions, you will not likely hold the power of inspiration well. And people will not likely trust you with it.

Overall, then, the positions of the powers in the pyramid show their sequence of development. The power of emotion, and its associated power of passion, must be developed before the power of inspiration. And the power of intellect, as it provides foundational credibility, must be sufficiently developed before any of the other powers can be effectively used. Each level in the pyramid assumes adequate development at the levels below it.

As shown in Figure 1.1, leaders who function at the bottom level of the pyramid provide what I call *Rational Leadership*. Their impact on others is primarily rational. People working under such leaders see logical reasons for doing what is asked of them. In this sense, they are motivated. But they are not excited or inspired. The next level, and a much more powerful one, is *Passionate Leadership*. Leaders at this level are effective in transforming negative emotions into positive ones. They unblock and activate

POWER TALK (to self)

- "At what level of the Four Powers Pyramid am I operating?"

- "To what extent do I truly move people to take action?"

passion that is potent fuel for driving their people and their visions forward. Naturally, those they lead are excited. The top level of the pyramid is *Inspirational Leadership*. Those who experience leaders operating at this high level are truly inspired.

At each next higher level in the pyramid, the leader's impact is greater. And, in parallel, other people's engagement is fuller. Higher levels of success naturally follow. In the subsequent chapters, you will learn how to ascend the pyramid and be more powerful.

summary

KEY POINTS TO REMEMBER

- The power within you consists of four separate capacities: the powers of intellect, passion, emotion, and inspiration. You can develop each of these powers to be ever more potent drivers of your success.

- Your power of intellect—your capacity to effectively use reason and logic—is necessary for "opening the door" and gaining credibility. But it is not enough. People are typically not moved by logic to take action.

- Your power of passion—the life energy that is demonstrated through your words and actions—enlivens you and will energize those around you as well.

- Negative emotions such as fear, anger, and self-doubt block your passion. Positive emotions such as excitement, exuberance, and joy express it.

- Your power of emotion—the capacity to be aware of and transform your emotions—enables you to unblock your passion and impact others in positive and potent ways.

- Your power of inspiration—the capacity to "bring spirit in"—equips you to provide people a galvanizing experience of being part of something greater than their separate selves.

- Each level in the Four Powers Pyramid assumes sufficient development of the powers below it.

ACTIONS TO ENHANCE YOUR POWER

- Take five minutes to reflect on your own development of each of the four powers. Where are you stronger? Where are you less developed? Pay particular attention to your power of emotion, as this is the power that is most likely limiting your degree of success. How well are you managing your emotional states? To what extent do feelings of inadequacy, fear, and anger impede you? Make some notes of your findings and keep them in mind as you read the chapters that follow. Because the power of emotion is so crucial for you, most of this book will be focused on helping you to develop it.

RECOGNIZE THE DIFFERENCES BETWEEN INTERNAL AND EXTERNAL POWER SO YOU CAN LEAD WISELY

You can magnetize others with the pull of your four internal powers. Alternatively, you can push them into action using the power that has its origins outside of you. For example, you can tell people what to do based on the authority of your role. This is sometimes necessary. But be cautious with your use of external power. People may feel controlled and coerced by you. If they do, they may covertly resist your control and repeatedly sabotage you in a silent underground war. Ultimately, you will be more powerful by growing your internal power rather than resorting to the push of your external power.

In the prior sections, we focused on the power that comes from the inside. Sometimes, you may also use power that has its source outside of you. For example, you may use the authority of your leadership position to require people to act as you direct. Your use of this type of power—*external power*—may sometimes be necessary. But be careful when you use it. The people you direct may feel controlled and even coerced. That is a danger to you.

> **definition**
>
> **EXTERNAL POWER**
> Power whose origin is outside of you, as opposed to the *internal* powers of intellect, passion, emotion, and inspiration.

When people feel controlled or forced, they often resist. They resist when they experience power being used *against* them, rather than *for* them or *with* them. This is human nature. And if they believe that resisting openly is too dangerous and susceptible to retaliation, as it often is, then their resistance will be hidden. Such covert resistance is rife within organizations. And it causes great harm.

One CEO hired me after he began to wonder whether his forceful style of leadership was working. When we first met, his office was dominated by a giant photo on an easel of a boxing match. Muhammad Ali was glaring and standing over Sonny Liston, whom he had just knocked out. As I looked at the photo and back at my client, I said, "I think you'd rather be a Muhammad Ali than a Sonny Liston."

"You betcha," he said. And then after a brief pause, he added, "I used to fight with my four brothers over a bowl of cereal in the morning."

Many years after fighting for his breakfast, he was now using a similarly forceful approach, relying on the authority of his position to push his employees hard for the results he wanted. The employees, though, resented this and were naturally resisting. My client had sensed the resistance and had warned that anyone "not 100 percent supporting our goals" would face dire consequences. The resistance did not stop; it just went underground. Then my client was faced with fighting an underground war.

Such resistance is sometimes called *passive-aggressive* behavior. It is true that people acting in this way are damaging themselves and their organizations. But rather than judging and blaming them, it is more powerful to not create resistance in the first place or, failing that, to convert it. So when you suspect people are resisting you, ask yourself, "What did I do to bring this about?

DEEPER WISDOM

Depending on their personalities and the particular circumstances, some people will feel personally diminished by succumbing to your forceful control. They would rather resist your leadership and fight a risky underground war than acquiesce and face the bigger risk of losing their sense of dignity. The more forceful you are, the more likely you are to trigger this dynamic that can harm you.

And how can I change it?" Asking such questions makes you more effective.

Have you ever fought an underground war—on either side? How much of your energy was diverted to that cause? How did that affect you—and those around you? Instead of pushing to make things happen as the executive did in the prior example, consider pulling instead.

Using the internal powers of your personality and developing them in the ways I'll show you, pull people into the orbit of your influence. Magnetize them with your passion, your boldness, and your caring. Create a reality where your people's efforts come from the pull of *"I want to"* rather than the push of *"I have to."*

This approach works outside the professional context as well. I used it with my nephew when he was five years old. His mother was telling him he "had to" go to bed. But he didn't want to. A dramatic power struggle erupted, with much yelling and tears. After a while, I simply reached out to my nephew, placed my palm on the center of his chest, and whispered, "Sammy, be powerful." He quietly stood up and walked upstairs to bed. His mother was astounded. She exclaimed, "How did you do that? I can't ever get him to do that!" I explained that I saw her use of external power was not working. So instead, I used my internal power. I showed my nephew how to be calm, caring, and strong all at the same time. In doing so, I activated the same capacities within him. I activated *his* internal power.

Your leadership—whether in a professional or a personal capacity—will likely be a combination of the pull of your internal power and the push of your external power. Ask yourself, though, which approach you want to be primary. Ask, "What type of leader do I want to be? Which approach will give me the greatest power?" You may notice that when you push too much, you create power struggles and underground conflicts. And that actually depletes your power.

The word *power* has a negative connotation for some people. They confuse it to mean the control, the force, and the coercion that some "push" leaders rely on in their attempts to be powerful. But true power does not necessarily imply these characteristics at all. True power is simply the capacity to make things happen. And as you'll see as we continue, that capacity has its greatest source within you.

KEY POINTS TO REMEMBER

- In addition to the internal powers of your intellect, passion, emotion, and inspiration, you have the power whose origin is external to you. An example of external power is the authority of your position.

- Relying too heavily on your external power may cause people to feel controlled and coerced by you. As a result, they may come to resist you. Typically, the resistance will be hidden.

- Such resistance is often called *passive-aggressive* behavior. But rather than attaching a label to those who resist you, it is better to understand the cause of their conduct so that you can change it.

- Your leadership will likely draw on a combination of internal and external power. Excessive reliance on external power, though, can ultimately be power-depleting. Therefore, be conscious and deliberate in your choice of which type of power to emphasize in your actions.

ACTIONS TO ENHANCE YOUR POWER

- Reflect on how you typically motivate action in those over whom you hold authority. Ask yourself, "To what extent might people feel pushed and controlled by me? Are any of them resisting me as a result?" If you sense any such resistance, then also ask yourself how you are responding to it. Depending on your answers, consider making a plan for leading differently.

- Think of the best bosses you've ever had—and the worst as well. What characteristics made them the best or worst? Were some of these qualities related to how they held and used their power? Based on their examples, identify what type of leader you wish to be. Write down the relevant qualities and commit to them.

EXPAND YOUR SELF-AWARENESS
TO EXPAND YOUR POWER

The choices you make either increase or decrease your power. Therefore, in every instance, choose the action that empowers you. So choosing will require you to be self-aware. Ideally, you will be aware of your actions, the emotions that trigger these actions, and the perceptions that, in turn, generate your emotions. To the extent your awareness is that encompassing, you will be well equipped to continuously make wise choices that empower you. If you expand your awareness further to include knowledge of how others perceive your actions, feel about them, and respond to them, you will have even greater capacity for acting wisely and effectively. All of this power-enhancing knowledge can be yours if you take the time to reflect, carefully observe, and skillfully ask others for feedback.

Every moment is a fork in the road. Every moment presents you a choice. Depending on how you choose, you will be more powerful or less so. In order to choose deliberately and effectively, you must be self-aware.

For example, you may not be aware of the signals you are sending to other people. And you may not be aware of how that is harming you. I worked with a leader who was frustrated that several of her peers were not supporting her. In telling me about the problem, she concluded, "They all went to the same business school, they're all in the same clique, and they don't care about anyone but themselves." Yet, as we explored further, it came out that she viewed these colleagues as less intelligent, less insightful, and ultimately less valuable than herself.

"Do you believe they are not sensing how you see them?" I asked. I further inquired whether she might be unintentionally telegraphing this in many subtle ways, including in the words she used, in her tone of voice, and even in her posture. My client came to the painful conclusion that her colleagues were likely experiencing her as arrogant and disdainful. She came to realize that she had created a mountain of resentment within them—and the very lack of cooperation of which she was complaining.

Once she had greater self-awareness, she could make different choices and create different outcomes. Ultimately, she found that the "clique" she was seeing was mostly a figment of her imagination. As one of these colleagues later told her after my client had repaired the relationship, "What we mostly had in common is that we thought you were full of yourself and wanted to run all over us." You can create better outcomes, too. When you are aware of what you are doing and how it's affecting others, you will often choose to act differently. That will change how others experience you and, therefore, how they respond to you. And that will have a profound impact on your degree of success.

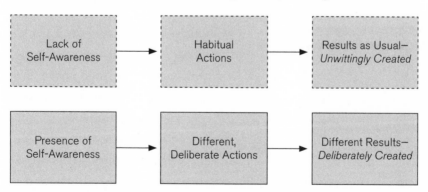

FIGURE 1.2 Impact of Self-Awareness on Results

Figure 1.2 illustrates this for you. The top diagram shows how events unfold when you are less than fully self-aware. You engage in certain habitual actions and unwittingly create certain unfavorable results. This is what happened in the previous example. The alternative, shown at the bottom of Figure 1.2, is expanding your self-awareness. This will cause you to act differently and thereby create different outcomes. In the first scenario, you are the victim of the results. You may ask, "Why me?" In the second scenario, the results are much more the product of your own deliberate choice.

When I talk with new clients about self-awareness, some of them say, "Dean, I'm pretty self-aware. I know what I'm doing." But what I typically find is something very different. As I interview their colleagues and as I observe them myself, I find a number of aspects of their conduct that they've been unaware of. They are surprised when they learn of these things. And often, these gaps in their self-awareness have been harming them greatly.

Such gaps in self-awareness are quite common. It's human nature to not see ourselves clearly. I too have many self-awareness gaps. Therefore, I frequently ask for others' observations about me. Sometimes, hearing that information can be painful. But it's better to find out earlier rather than later how I'm hurting myself. Perhaps I'll discover that I'm coming across as too opinionated. Or that I'm giving away my power. Or that I'm irritating a colleague. I need to know these things as soon as possible.

POWER TALK (to self)

- "What am I not seeing about myself?"
- "What do others notice about me that I'm missing?"

How about you? How soon do you want to find out how you are harming yourself? How you are diminishing your power? Do you really know how people are experiencing you? Consider taking steps now to enhance your self-awareness. Consider asking yourself, "What am I not seeing about myself? What do others see about me that I don't see?" Asking such questions will render you more powerful. Even better is directly asking your colleagues for their observations of you. At the end of this section, I'll show you how to do this most effectively. But first, let's identify all that self-awareness includes.

At a minimum, your self-awareness requires being cognizant of your actions. Yet many people frequently lack even this level of awareness. I worked with an executive for a nonprofit who didn't realize that when his peers expressed views contrary to his own, the corners of his mouth would turn downward in a frown and his eyes would narrow. His colleagues told me they were therefore limiting their communication with him. When I conveyed all this to my client, he rather flatly responded, "I'm not aware I do that." He seemed to be disagreeing with me. I said, "You're doing it right now." He was startled. Gaining self-awareness can be disturbing, but this is often what enables us to start acting differently and more effectively.

Your expansion in awareness need not stop with knowledge of your actions. You will be even more effective and powerful when you know what is *driving* your conduct. And typically, what drives conduct, especially when it's

> **POWER TALK (to self)**
>
> - "Why am I acting this way?"
> - "What emotions are driving me to do this?"

ineffective, is emotion. So as you become more aware of behaviors you indulge in that are not working for you, ask yourself, "Why am I doing this? What emotions are causing me to act this way?"

In my conversation with the nonprofit executive, I asked him to resume the facial expression I'd just pointed out to him. When he did so, I asked, "With that expression, what are you feeling right now?" He replied, "Irritated, angry, and bored." "Is that what you feel," I inquired, "when people disagree with you?" "Yeah, I guess so," he answered with some amazement. "I hadn't realized that." Now that he knew what was triggering his actions, he had a greater capacity to act differently. Rather than reacting automatically to his emotions in ways that harmed him and his relationships, he could choose a different and more effective course of action.

You can expand your self-awareness yet one step further. Once you know the triggering emotion, you can ask, "But what is causing this feel-

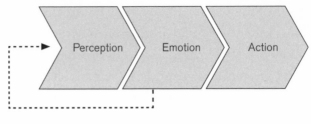

FIGURE 1.3 PEA Chain

ing to arise?" Knowing the answer will provide you more information for making a better choice. It will provide you an additional increase in your power. And what typically triggers your emotions are perceptions.

Your perceptions are how you see people and their conduct and the events around you. Perceptions include your beliefs and assumptions. The sequence, then, as shown in Figure 1.3, is that your perceptions trigger your emotions and your emotions trigger your actions. So your perceptions play a very powerful role in your personality. They set in motion chain reactions—what I call PEA (Perception–Emotion–Action) chains— that are often outside your awareness.

> **definition**
>
> **PERCEPTION**
> Your *subjective* understanding of other people's actions and the events around you. It includes your beliefs and assumptions.

You will benefit greatly by always remembering one key characteristic of your perceptions: They are not necessarily true. Quite often, in fact, they are false or at least so incomplete as to mislead you. Your perceptions are not objective reality. Rather, they are your interpretation of reality.

For example, you are angry with a colleague for disrespecting you. You infer her disrespect from the fact that she avoids you. But you may be misreading the signals. Her avoidance of you may actually be due to her misperception that you don't, in fact, respect her. So both you and your colleague are acting on complementary misperceptions of each other. Paired misperceptions like this are very common—and they generate great amounts of unnecessary anger.

28 PRINCIPLES OF POWER

Examine closely, therefore, those situations in which you are having negative reactions to others. Identify your perceptions—your beliefs and assumptions—that give rise to your negative reactions. How do you know those perceptions are true?

The nonprofit executive I mentioned earlier was angry when people disagreed with him. But what perception, I wondered with him, was driving these feelings? We found it was his belief that his peers were attacking him and belittling his ideas. "Are you sure that is always what's happening when your colleagues disagree with you?" I asked. "No, of course not," he replied. He reflected for a moment and added, "Wow, I've really been caught up in my own personality."

As we uncovered additional beliefs, I encouraged my client to get more curious. I asked him, "Are there different ways to see these things? Are different perceptions possible?" I encourage you to get curious, too. Things are rarely as they seem.

Be careful, then, about what stories you tell yourself. Your perceptions are subjective and may not be true. And their inherent subjectivity is intensified by the fact that your emotions filter and flavor them. So even as your perceptions determine your emotions, your emotions also partly determine your perceptions. This is the reason for the dashed line in Figure 1.3 going from emotion back to perception. Each actually influences the other.

For example, if you are angry with a colleague, you are likely to view all her actions through an anger lens. You are therefore likely to misconstrue her actions in a way that further fuels your anger. And that greater degree of anger will distort your perceptions even more. It is a vicious cycle that disempowers you.

> **DEEPER WISDOM**
>
> People perceive the same events in remarkably divergent ways. This is due to many subjective factors, such as their emotional states, their needs, their likes and dislikes, and their histories. Therefore, if you are similar to most people, you have thick filters that color and distort your perceptions. As you become more aware of these filters, they will have less control over you. Then you will be able to see more clearly and navigate through your environment more effectively.

So every time you have a negative emotional reaction, ask yourself, "What is causing me to feel this way? What am I believing? What am I assuming?" Then ask, "Am I certain these beliefs and assumptions are true? Can I see things differently?" These are very helpful questions to ask. They will empower you. Be careful, then, not to believe everything you think. If you knew all there is to know about any person or issue, almost certainly your opinion would be different.

Now that you know about PEA (Perception–Emotion–Action) chains, consider using them often as a tool to enhance your self-awareness. First, identify the actions that are impeding your effectiveness and thereby blocking your power. Then identify the emotions driving those actions. And then identify the underlying perceptions. By doing so, you can intervene at any step in what is otherwise an unconscious process. You can change your perceptions, you can change your emotions, and you can change your actions. And as you change your actions, people will respond to you differently. In this way, you can dramatically enhance your power.

When you are unhappy with how things are going for you, consider even diagramming your relevant PEA chains. Once they are so visible, staring back at you, it may be difficult for you to continue indulging the same old patterns. Then you can take the necessary steps to restore more of your freedom and more of your power.

So far, we have been focusing on the chain of causation inside of you. In addition to the internal PEA chain, there is an external one as well. As shown in Figure 1.4, your actions generate perceptions in other people. And those perceptions generate emotions that, in turn, trigger actions. As you expand your self-awareness to include this impact you have on others, you will become more astute in activating the responses you desire.

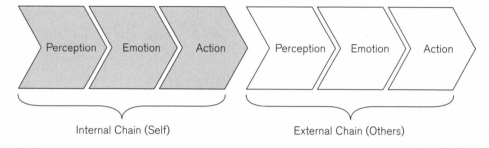

Internal Chain (Self) External Chain (Others)

FIGURE 1.4 Expanded PEA Chain

For example, I worked with a leader whose boss repeatedly and vigorously challenged her strategy. My client's perception was, "Even though I had thought my strategy was excellent, my boss appears to think it is misguided." As a result, she felt fear and self-doubt. Acting on these emotions, she repeatedly adjusted her strategy in an effort to satisfy her boss. This triggered a perception in him: "My direct report lacks the conviction of her beliefs. I challenge her and she capitulates. How can I trust her?" The boss's consequent emotions were fear and irritation. This triggered yet more challenges by him. And his subordinate kept on failing these tests. She was not accurately interpreting his challenges to her.

Once my client was able to correctly read the full PEA chain—the part internal to her and the external part within her boss—she was able to choose a more powerful course of action. She started standing by her strategy and defending it against her boss's challenges. He was gratified and relieved that she was back in her power.

Using PEA chains in this way, you can logically take apart and understand every one of your interactions and relationships that do not go well. In order to do this effectively, though, you need the relevant information. You need to know which of your actions are limiting your success. And you need to know the chain of perceptions, emotions, and actions your conduct is triggering in other people. Your self-reflection and careful observation may not be enough to gather all of this crucial data.

Therefore, gathering feedback from others will be essential for you. Yet, your colleagues may be reluctant to share their observations. They may worry how you will receive their input. They may be concerned about damaging their relationships with you. So when you ask for their feedback, pose your questions skillfully, in a way that invites a meaningful response. And show your sincere interest in receiving whatever they may provide you.

So do not ask, for example, "How'd I do in the meeting?" You will likely get a brief response like "Fine" or "You did great." Such a response may give you a vague sense of reassurance. But it does not help you in expanding your self-awareness and therefore your power. It is better to ask, "How could I have been more effective in that meeting?" Consider adding, "I'm really interested to know." If you want more information, ask, "If I were the perfect VP of Sales [or whatever your role is], what would I be doing differently?" Consider also asking, "How do people perceive me? How do they feel about me?" Some of the responses you get will pertain to other people. And much of it will be about how the speaker himself sees you and feels about you.

> **POWER TALK (to others)**
>
> - "How could I have been more effective in that meeting?"
> - "Tell me two things I could have done better."
> - "How am I being perceived?"

As you consider asking questions such as these, you will likely fear what you may discover. That fear is common and natural, but don't let it stop you. If you are willing to push through your fear, you will gain a crucial expansion of your self-awareness—and therefore of your power.

You may also be concerned that asking for feedback will make you appear unsure of yourself. But that is not a danger, provided you ask your questions from a position of confident power rather than from a position of self-doubt. The greater danger is seeking too little feedback and therefore operating without information vital for your greater success.

KEY POINTS TO REMEMBER

- As you increase your self-awareness, you increase your capacity to make wise choices that enhance your effectiveness and therefore your power. On the other hand, to the extent you lack self-awareness, your actions will tend to be automatic, habitual, and less effective.

- Seek to expand your self-awareness to include each of the following steps in your internal Perception–Emotion–Action (PEA) chains:

  - Your *actions*

  - The *emotions* that trigger your actions

  - The *perceptions* that, in turn, generate your emotions

- Ideally, your self-awareness will extend even further to include the external PEA chains that your actions activate in others.

- You can learn the specifics of your internal and external PEA chains through your continuous use of self-reflection, careful observation, and skillful requests for feedback.

ACTIONS TO ENHANCE YOUR POWER

- Set aside a half-hour at the end of every week to self-reflect. During that time, identify two or three instances during the week in which your emotions took control of you or you otherwise acted in a way that was ineffective. For each such instance, identify the specific ineffective actions, the triggering emotions, and the perceptions that gave rise to them. Diagram these internal PEA chains as well as the apparent reactions you activated in others (the external PEA chains). Ask yourself, "Were my initial perceptions that triggered these chain reactions necessarily true? What other ways of seeing things might have yielded better results?"

- Commence a practice of regularly seeking feedback. Start by approaching two colleagues you trust and ask them for feedback concerning an event in which you just performed. Ask, for example:

  - How could I have been more effective?

  - How was I perceived?

  - What do you sense were people's reactions to me?

2

· THE POWER OF EMOTION ·
MASTER THE FORCES THAT MOVE THE MIND AND HEART

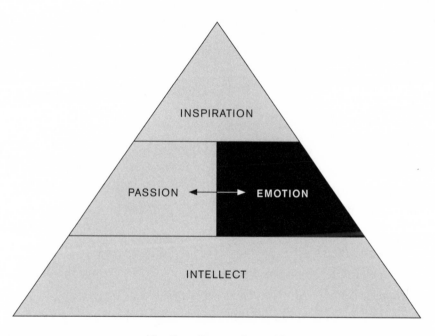

The Four Powers Pyramid

TRANSFORM YOUR NEGATIVE EMOTIONS
TO UNBLOCK YOUR PASSION

Your fear, anger, and self-doubt are natural, especially if you are a leader. Yet, they are blocking your power and damaging your relationships. You may be tempted to push these feelings out of awareness and act as if they were not present. Doing so will only make them stronger. Then they will control your actions without your knowledge. The only powerful thing to do with negative emotions is to transform them.

Negative emotions are natural and predictable for nearly all people. Fear, anger, and feelings of inadequacy are especially common, and all the more so for leaders, given their many stressors. You will likely find they are common in you too. This is not a problem by itself, but if you allow these feelings to linger and govern your actions, they will harm you greatly. They will block your power and damage your relationships.

For example, if you fear a painful but necessary change in your life or in your organization and then act on your fear by resisting it, you will have limited your capacity. You will have dissipated your power as a person and as a leader. If you feel inadequate and act on your self-doubt by failing to pursue opportunities for your greater growth and fulfillment, you will have blocked your power in that way as well. And if you resent a colleague or friend and act on your anger by avoiding her, you will have damaged your relationship and blocked your power again.

So ask yourself, "How do I act on my negative emotions? Where have my fear, anger, and self-doubt undermined my relationships?

Where have they impaired my leadership?" If you look closely, you will likely identify many such instances. With the information I will provide you, you will be able to free yourself from these power-depleting patterns. You can transform any negative emotion into a positive one. You can transform any fear into courage, any anger into compassion, any shame into dignity, and any feelings of disconnection into relatedness.

Many people, though, take a very different approach. Rather than challenging their negative emotions head-on, they ignore them and pretend they're not present. Should you do this, your emotions will not disappear. Hidden beneath the surface, they will fester and grow stronger. And because you are not aware of them, they will be less subject to your control as they govern your thoughts, words, and actions. Likely, others will still sense them even if you don't. And they will respond to you accordingly.

POWER TALK (to self)
• "Where are my fear, anger, and self-doubt harming my relationships?"
• "Where are they blocking my power?"

For example, you may not like getting angry, so you disregard those feelings when they arise within you. But unbeknownst to you, your resentments probably still leak out indirectly. Your colleagues and family members likely sense these feelings in how you speak to them, or avoid them. If this is happening, you are harming your relationships with the very people you need. And it is all outside your awareness.

I was asked to work with a business manager whom colleagues described as often angry and resentful. "But I hardly ever get angry," he insisted. To address the disparity in viewpoints, I showed him what his peers were saying. One, for example, described him as sitting through meetings in a removed silence as if to telegraph, "Why do I have to waste my time here?" Another colleague complained that she had tediously labored for months to create a conclusive report, but he ignored her requests that he review it and send her his comments. Then, after the report was already final, he dismissed it as a "first draft" in a large and open forum.

"Do you recognize any of what they're saying?" I asked. "Yeah," he said, "but I don't think any of this makes me an angry person." "Do some meetings feel like an unwise use of your time?" I inquired. "Actually, some meetings are a pretty huge waste of my time," he replied. "But that doesn't irritate you?" I asked. "Well, just a little," he responded. "How about the one where you called the big report a 'first draft'?" "Well, she just annoys me," he said. "Who else annoys you?" I asked.

By the time we finished talking, this manager realized he had many resentments—and that people were detecting them and reacting accordingly. The poison he was spewing was beginning to come back at him. Perhaps he was a bit outside the norm, but could you be somewhat similar? Could you be having a similar impact on at least some people?

Or perhaps the larger challenge for you is your self-doubt rather than your anger. You may prefer to see yourself as confident, ignoring the feelings of inadequacy that gnaw at you. Yet, those feelings may still control you. When you respond to a colleague, they may emerge in the form of defensive self-justifications when, really, none are necessary. Or these feelings may hold you back from providing your own impassioned views when, in fact, your input is needed.

Only by addressing your negative emotions directly can you avoid such conduct that dissipates your power. Your most powerful response to your negative emotions is not to ignore them, but to transform them.

Occasionally, your emotions are valid signals of a situation that requires your urgent attention. For example, your fear may be signaling that a car is about to collide with you or that a colleague really is seeking to harm you. Your self-doubt may be appropriately telling you that you lack the skills necessary for your role and should promptly seek out the necessary training. And your expressed anger may be an appropriate means of stopping someone's repeated intrusions into your domain.

However, such situations are much more the exception than the rule. Typically, your negative emotions are based on distorted perceptions. Typically, acting on these feelings renders you less effective. Therefore, it will serve you to transform them before they take control of you and harm you. In the following section, I will provide you a map for making these transformations and preserving your power.

summary

KEY POINTS TO REMEMBER

- Negative emotions such as fear, anger, and feelings of inadequacy are very common in people, including leaders. Therefore, they are likely common in you as well.

- If you act on these emotions, they will harm you. They will damage your relationships and impede your effectiveness.

- If, on the other hand, you ignore these feelings, they will not go away. Instead, they will grow stronger and govern your actions without your even knowing it.

- Therefore, your most powerful response to negative emotions is not to act on them or to ignore them. Rather, it is to transform them into positive emotions.

ACTIONS TO ENHANCE YOUR POWER

- Set aside ten minutes. Of these three groups of emotions—(1) your fears and anxieties, (2) your resentments and irritations, (3) your self-doubts and feelings of inadequacy—choose the one that seems most prominent within you. Then reflect on the following two questions: "How have these emotions recently harmed me personally and professionally? What would be different in my life and career right now if I did not act on those feelings?" To make this exercise more powerful for you, record your answers in writing.

USE THE FIVE GIFTS ROADMAP AS A
NAVIGATIONAL TOOL FOR GOVERNING
YOUR EMOTIONAL STATES

For every one of the major emotional states that deplete your power, there is a corresponding positive state into which it can be transformed. The Five Gifts Roadmap will assist you in making these transformations. It will help you identify your current negative state and then show you its positive, corresponding emotion. If you choose to not transform your negative state, the Roadmap will also show you the next negative emotion you'll likely fall into. Each time you transform your negative state into a positive one, you enhance your power. And every time you descend into another negative emotion, your life and your leadership are diminished.

Five different types of emotional states can harm you. As a person and as a leader, you likely experience each of them at times. I call these states *poisons* because of the destructive impact they can have on you and your environment. Each, in fact, represents a profound danger to you. Yet, you can transform each poison into its corresponding *gift*. These are gifts because they can be so beneficial to you and those you lead. The Five Gifts Roadmap at Figure 2.1 shows you the five poisons and the corresponding five gifts into which they can be transformed.

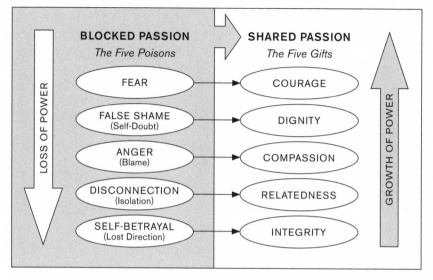

FIGURE 2.1 The Five Gifts Roadmap

The first three poisons are emotions. They are fear, feelings of self-doubt—what I call *false shame*—and anger. The next two poisons are emotionally driven states. They are disconnection from others and self-betrayal. The latter means betrayal of your mission in life and your values, and, ultimately, your betrayal of others.

As the Five Gifts Roadmap shows, you can transform each of these poisons. You can transform your fear into courage. You can transform your false shame and self-doubt into dignity. And you can transform your anger into compassion. Further down on the Roadmap, you can transform your disconnection into relatedness and your self-betrayal into a deeper sense of your own integrity. Each of these transformations will render you a more powerful person and a more effective leader. I will show you how to produce each of them in the following five chapters.

I could say I "created" the Five Gifts Roadmap, but really, I only discovered a set of fundamental human principles that have long been recognized in many cultures and traditions. I made these discoveries out of sheer necessity. At an earlier point in my life, I was struggling through a very dark time and suffering greatly, and I didn't know why. To climb out of the hole I was in, I had to discover what was causing my unhappiness. As I looked inside, I saw each of the five poisons.

I discovered how my fear was keeping me stuck and unable to take the bold actions my personal and professional life required. I saw how my false shame was feeding me messages that I was inadequate and unworthy and therefore unable to create the changes I needed. I observed how my resentments were preoccupying me and poisoning me. And then I came to see how this mass of negative emotion was disconnecting me from others. And finally, I saw that these states were causing me to betray my own values and purpose in life.

Seeing all this, I understood why I was feeling helpless and powerless. I saw how each of these poisons was depleting my power. And knowing the cause, then I could know the cure. I knew I had to take back my power. So, for each poison, I found the antidote—the corresponding gift state into which each poison could be transformed. Through that transformational work, I was able to restore much of my power.

I am not now entirely free of the poison states. Almost no one ever really is. These poisons still arise within me, and if I am not careful, one or more of them will take over my mood and my actions. For example, I may let fear set in and stop me from taking the next crucial steps in my professional life. Or I may let a certain irritability take control and then I'll feel alienated from some of those around me.

When this happens, when I feel out of my power, I look at the Roadmap posted on the wall above my desk. Even though I have it memorized by now, I still sometimes look and ask myself, "Where am I now?" Consider doing the same. Consider using the Roadmap as a navigational tool that tells you where you are now and where you want to go. Especially when you feel depleted in your power, ask yourself, "What negative state am I in now?" After locating the poison on the Roadmap that is active within you in that moment, locate its corresponding gift state. Then, using the instructions in the following five chapters, make the necessary transformation.

Continuously following these steps will awaken you out of any state of powerlessness you have fallen into. And then you can navigate to the right side of the Roadmap and reclaim your power.

Now you have at least a beginning sense of how to use the horizontal dimension of the Roadmap. Using the Roadmap in this way, you move from left to right to transform each poison into its corresponding gift. You can use the vertical dimension of the Roadmap as well. That dimension shows you the likely sequencing of your negative emotional states if you are not careful. On the left side of the Roadmap, it is indicated by the "Loss of Power" arrow pointing downward.

Knowing the vertical dimension, you can determine where you are in the sequence of your emotions and where you may go next unless you take back your power. This sequence does not describe every person in every situation. But in my work with leaders, I have found this sequence to be the most typical. It may or may not be typical for you. For example, you may often go directly from false shame to disconnection, skipping the usual step of anger. Or the first negative emotion you experience may be a feeling of inadequacy rather than fear. So as you read about the vertical dimension, ask yourself, "How does this sequence of emotional states fit me? What is unique about how I move from one negative state to another?"

Regardless of your uniqueness, the very first step in your sequence of negative emotions is actually a perception. It is a distorted perception—

a false belief—of either partial or complete powerlessness. You will see yourself as less powerful than you actually are. On the Roadmap, this is called "blocked passion."

For example, you may secretly believe that you don't have "what it takes" to excel in your current professional role. Or you may believe that you cannot significantly affect how people respond to you. These perceptions may have some truth in them. Likely, though, as in most such cases, they are more distortion than reality. With these perceptions, you are saying, in effect, "I am powerless to really shine in my role" or "I am powerless to change how people see me." And those statements are mostly untrue.

Notice what happens when you begin to feel powerless. Don't you begin to feel fear—the first of the five poisons—too? That, in fact, is the usual sequence. But you have a choice with your fear. You can transform it into courage by taking action despite what it tells you. Or you can descend down the Roadmap into the next poison and therefore into a greater loss of power. You have this same choice for each of the poisons until you reach the bottom. You can transform the poison into its corresponding gift and therefore be more powerful. Or you can descend to the next poison and thereby go into greater powerlessness. The increased powerlessness results because each negative emotion you experience weakens you and makes you less effective.

So if you do not transform your fear into courage, you will likely descend into the next poison, false shame. This is because living in a state of fear undermines your self-esteem. Retreating in the face of your anxieties instead of overcoming them predictably triggers feelings of inadequacy.

This was the case for an introverted public official early in her career. When she would attend functions at which powerful decision-makers were present, she'd feel intimidated and hold back rather than seek ways to meet them. But success in her role required her to get more connected. She explained to me, "My shrinking back was destroying my self-confidence. Sometimes, I'd end up standing alone in the middle of the room at those events, not knowing what to do with myself, feeling completely awkward and embarrassed."

She is now quite different. When I observed her at one event, she moved with grace and poise as she mingled with the guests. "I realized," she said, "that if I didn't defeat my fear, it was going to defeat me. So I made it my goal for each function to talk with the people who most scared me. And the more I did that, the more confident I became." She is now a senior government official and mentors young colleagues with similar challenges.

> **POWER TALK (to self)**
>
> • "Looking at the Roadmap, what poison might I go to next if I don't take back my power and transform my negative state right now?"

Should you find yourself feeling inadequate and unworthy, know that this is actually a very common experience for leaders. And bear in mind that these feelings, like all the five poisons, are based on a distortion of reality. I use the term "false shame" because if you could see your own true worth, you would never have any feelings of shame or inadequacy.

When false shame and self-doubt arise, you have a choice here as well. You can transform that state into dignity. Or you can descend into anger, the next poison. Anger ensues at this point because it typically originates in feelings of inadequacy. When you feel self-doubt, you are more vulnerable to feeling disrespected and offended by people's actions. You are more likely, therefore, to get angry. The self-blame of false shame becomes the blaming of others typical of anger. The ashamed voice of "I am inadequate" becomes the angry voice of "You are inadequate."

For example, you may sometimes feel inadequate when a prospective client or employer decides to not use your services. What do you do with those feelings? Do you, like many people, convert them into some degree of anger? Or maybe you can remember a time when an intimate partner rejected you and you felt not good enough and unworthy. Did you not then also get angry? Or perhaps there have been times when you were driving your car—or your business—and briefly got lost and started doubting yourself. Did you feel your irritation well up when someone beside you began questioning your direction? As you will see, such manifestations of anger undermine your effectiveness and deplete your power.

You have a choice when feeling angry, too. You can transform that state into compassion. Or you can descend into further powerlessness, into a state of disconnection and increasing isolation. Disconnection naturally arises at this stage because your feeling badly about yourself, and particularly your anger, drives a wedge between you and those around you. More broadly, your mix of fear, false shame, and anger at this point will likely create a distance between you and others. Positive emotions usually bring people together. Negative ones usually pull them apart.

This disconnection will be a significant danger for you. To the extent you are cut off from people and the support they can provide you, you are deprived of much of your power.

When disconnected, your choice is to transform that into relatedness or to drop down to the bottom poison, self-betrayal. This is the most power-depleting poison because at this point, you betray what is most important for you. You may betray your fundamental values, your mission and purpose in life, and even your relationships. It may feel like a nagging sense that your actions are not consistent with who you truly are and what you stand for.

Self-betrayal is such a profound danger to you because to the extent you are not true to yourself, you are cut off from the core of your power. Yet even at this point, you can choose to transform your self-betrayal into integrity. And in this way, you begin your upward climb toward reclaiming your full power.

Self-betrayal is more common than you likely realize. If you look closely, perhaps you can remember times when you were so overcome with negative emotions that you started avoiding your colleagues, your friends, or your spouse. Then, deprived of their support, perhaps you engaged in behaviors that, ultimately, felt unsettling and harmful for you. Instead of condemning yourself for these instances, learn from them. They are a common element of the human condition. They are also a common part of many great leaders' biographies. You can protect yourself from self-betrayal by detecting the poisons and transforming them before they lead you to that final destination.

Be mindful, then, how you can fall down and get caught in the sequence of the five poisons. Be mindful of their dangers. If you are not self-aware and careful to hold your power, you can quickly cascade downward and find yourself in an unhappy and power-depleted place. But even if you find yourself at the bottom, you can climb back up again. By following the instructions in the following chapters and transforming each of the poisons in turn, you can take back your power.

To take that transformational journey, follow the "Growth of Power" arrow pointing upward on the right side of the Roadmap. Start wherever you are and work your way up. If you find yourself at the bottom, start by transforming your self-betrayal into integrity. With your integrity intact, you then have the necessary foundation for moving back into relatedness. Then you will be able to better understand others and move into a state of compassion. Having compassion for others helps you have compassion for yourself and thereby reclaim your dignity. And with that intact, you will have an enhanced capacity for taking action despite your fear and thereby restoring your courage.

Use the Five Gifts Roadmap, then, as a tool for navigating your emotional states. Whenever you sense you are out of your full power, check

> **DEEPER WISDOM**
>
> Many people feel tormented and besieged by their negative emotions. But you can choose a more powerful stance. Consider welcoming your fear, anger, and self-doubt as opportunities for you to grow stronger. Consider greeting them as respected athletic opponents who will help you hone your transformational skill. With this mindset, you will be less caught up in your emotions. You will already be showing yourself that you are "larger" than they are.

the Roadmap and identify your location. Then choose to move to the right side of the map. Choose to transform the negative state you're in to reclaim your power. In so doing, you will be a more effective and capable leader.

summary

KEY POINTS TO REMEMBER

- At various times, you are likely to experience any one of five major negative states, each of which will impair your effectiveness. They are fear, self-doubt (false shame), anger, disconnection, and self-betrayal.

- Each of these negative states, called "poisons," originates in a mistaken belief of partial or complete powerlessness. Typically, these poisons then actually deplete your power, especially when you act on them.

- The poisons have corresponding positive states, called "gifts," into which they can be transformed. Fear can be transformed into courage, false shame into dignity, anger into compassion, disconnection into relatedness, and self-betrayal into integrity.

- Use the Five Gifts Roadmap to navigate through your negative states. The Roadmap will help you to identify your current state and will then present you with your two choices. One choice will be to transform the poison into its corresponding gift and thereby enhance your power. Your other choice will be to descend to the next poison and thereby move into greater powerlessness.

ACTIONS TO ENHANCE YOUR POWER

- Over the course of the next week, every time you feel less than fully energized or feel that your passion is not freely flowing, look at the Five Gifts Roadmap. Identify where you are. You may see that there are two or three or more of the poisons operating simultaneously. This is not uncommon. Then notice the corresponding gift states into which your active poisons can be transformed. Sometimes, the mere noticing can be quite helpful. In the chapters that follow, I will provide you the necessary instructions for effectively making these transformations.

YOUR FIRST STEP IN TRANSFORMING YOUR NEGATIVE EMOTIONS IS TO ACCEPT THEM

If you wish to transform your fear, anger, and false shame, first accept them. This does not mean you let them take over and govern your actions. Rather, it means that you acknowledge these states without self-criticism and self-condemnation. Your acceptance will be easier if you remember these states are only temporary and do not define you. Then you will less likely get ensnared by them. If, instead, you judge yourself for your negative states and fight them, you will only be feeding them and they will grow stronger. Your kind and compassionate self-acceptance will help disarm your negative emotions and therefore provide you more power.

Once you become aware of a negative emotion active within you, your first task is to accept it. Only then can you bring about its transformation. This may seem like a paradox, but you have to accept where you are now in order to get to where you want to go.

Your acceptance does not mean resignation. It does not mean you are giving up. And very importantly, it does not mean you are letting your negative states take control and govern your actions. It only means that you are acknowledging the presence of a certain emotion and are at peace with it, even while you endeavor to transform it.

Alternatively, if you do not accept your fear, anger, and self-doubt, you will be at war with them. The more fiercely you fight, the more entrenched they will become. And in your battling against these emotions, you will generate even more of them. For example, if you do not accept your fear but fight it instead, you may become angry with yourself for being fearful. Or you may become ashamed of your fear or even fearful of your fear. Similarly, you may get ashamed of your anger, angry at your shame, and so on.

A colleague explained this point to me many years ago. I was struggling with anxiety about speaking in front of large groups of people. I asked for his advice and he suggested that I accept my nervousness. I was very annoyed with this answer. I nearly shouted back at him, "I *cannot* accept it! I have to change it!" Over time, I had to see for myself this approach was not working. It only intensified my fear and I got more trapped in it. Finally, I stopped fighting so hard and came to a point where I accepted the fear. And then I became greater than it. I was no longer ensnared by it.

This will happen for you too. When you accept your fear or anger or self-doubt, it will grow smaller and you will grow larger. No longer locked in battle with it, you will be freer of it.

> **POWER TALK (to self)**
>
> • "I am not my emotions."
> • "Whatever I'm feeling now will soon go away."

It will be easier for you to accept your feelings of anger, inadequacy, and fear if you keep in mind they are only passing states rather than things that define you. So you need not define yourself with a statement such as, "I am an angry person." Instead, you can simply conclude you are a person temporarily feeling anger.

Your emotions are like the weather, always changing. They are like clouds that temporarily block the sun. If you observe closely, you will notice that they usually last only a very short time. So you can say to yourself, "I am not my emotions. Whatever I'm feeling now, I won't be feeling later." A stance like this gives you more freedom and more power.

One very successful executive struggled for years with feelings of inadequacy and low self-confidence. It was partly because she grew up in a culture where her skin color was darker than the norm. When she arrived for her first day of school as a young girl, the children called her "dirty duck" and then all moved to the other side of the room.

Now, many years later, in our first meeting, I noticed that she worked hard to be perfect in nearly every aspect of her appearance. It was her way of trying to make up for her feelings of inadequacy. Her clothes were perfect, her speech was perfect—even her mannerisms were perfect. It was especially important to her to *look* confident. But deep down, she wasn't confident. And so when any of her insecurity showed through, she was mortified. She felt ashamed for feeling shame because, as she told herself, she *should* be confident.

As we worked together, she came to see that her old feelings of impaired self-worth were entirely unfounded. Accordingly, they began to release their hold on her. Still, though, they would arise from time to time, like brief periods of rain. But when they did, she would no longer lapse into yet more shame about them. Instead, she would simply notice them with a kind attention. She would say to herself, "Oh, that's my irrational self-doubt again." And then she might even laugh. She was no longer ashamed of the feelings of inadequacy. Being amused by them, she was freer of them.

Accepting yourself and your emotions as this executive did requires you to be kind and compassionate with yourself. You might even say, "Oh, this fear is really hard for me. I see I am really struggling." This compassion actually strengthens you. It provides you the support you would feel if a colleague treated you with the same kindness. Alternatively, if you harshly judge and criticize yourself for your negative states, you will feel the same as if a colleague treated you that way. And then you might feel ashamed, beaten down, and angry. Those feelings will only harm you.

Therefore, when you become aware of your negative states, do not criticize or condemn yourself for them. And do not harshly reject them. You need not be the person who angrily yells, "I'm not angry!" Or the person who nervously stammers, "I'm not afraid." Instead, notice your state with a kind attention. In a friendly way, say to yourself, "Oh, there I go again." And then you might even smile. And then you can add, "Let's see if I can transform this state I'm in." Acting in these ways, you will be more powerful. You will be claiming greater power over your destructive emotions.

summary

KEY POINTS TO REMEMBER

- Accepting your fear, anger, and self-doubt is a crucial first step in transforming them. If, instead, you fight these states, they are likely to grow stronger and you will get more ensnared by them.

- Your transformation of your negative emotions will be aided when you remember they are only temporary and ever changing, like the weather, and do not define you.

- Your acceptance means you are being kind and compassionate with yourself. Such compassion will help you greatly in changing your negative emotions.

ACTIONS TO ENHANCE YOUR POWER

- Identify which of your negative emotions are most difficult for you to accept. What do you tell yourself when they arise? What effect do these reactions have on your negative states? Write down what you discover. Are your reactions helping? Or do they only cause you to feel worse? Depending on what you learn, consider trying a different and more compassionate approach.

TO BETTER MASTER YOUR NEGATIVE EMOTIONS, KNOW HOW THEY CIRCULATE AMONG PEOPLE

Emotions naturally and rapidly spread from person to person. This intensifies your challenge to master them. Sometimes, the passing of emotions happens simply by virtue of their contagious nature. And sometimes, because negative emotions are difficult to bear alone, the passing is actually intended. Either way, be careful and alert lest you get "infected"—or become a propagator of negativity yourself. Hold your power even as anger, self-doubt, and fear swirl around you. This will make you more effective as a person and as a leader.

Your challenge to master fear, anger, and self-doubt is heightened by their tendency to propagate between people and across organizations. Emotions, in fact, are highly contagious. Therefore, without any intention on their part to do so, people feeling negative emotions can cause you to feel them, too.

For example, one angry colleague at a meeting can create an angry atmosphere. Then others at the meeting, including you, may begin to feel angry, too. Dynamics such as this help create a distinct emotional climate within each organization—and within each family as well.

Some organizational and family climates are positive and energizing. Others are negative and disheartening.

I once visited a neighbor for a barbecue and soon noticed that the family was somewhat unrestrained in expressing their emotions. As I sat down next to their little girl and we started talking, she told me of her difficulties completing her second-grade homework. I offered what I thought might be an explanation. "Well, your house is kind of noisy," I said. She replied, "Everyone is yelling and screaming, so I just start yelling and screaming, too." I couldn't help but think of the parallels with some organizations I've observed, although the yelling there is typically the silent kind and much more subtle.

So be alert lest you "catch" someone else's negative emotions. And be careful that you do not spread these states yourself. Given the visibility and influence of leaders, their emotional states are especially contagious among others. If you are a leader, this places a special responsibility on you. Others will carefully attend to how well you meet this challenge. Your power will increase or decrease accordingly.

An executive I consulted to was remarkable in how consistently positive and upbeat she remained in the midst of her organization's dire financial hardships. Yet, in a brief moment of intense frustration, she complained in a meeting, "The senior leadership has to get off their butts and get us the resources we need." Because of this, she was denied a much-desired promotion.

I didn't need to suggest the underlying rationale for the decision, as she already understood. She explained, "The people in this organization look to me to be confident and composed. In the statement I made, I was powerless and angry. We can't afford to let that become the model of how we show up here." She got the promotion 18 months later.

Avoiding the overt display of your negative emotions, though, is not enough. If they are present within you, they will still be contagious. People will sense your feelings. You cannot help but communicate them in the subtleties of your gestures, postures, and facial expressions. One way or another, you give off the signals. And the people around you read them. And then they may adopt your emotional state—and put it into action. Therefore, your challenge includes not lingering in your negative feelings lest they spread and cause harm.

You can make the contagiousness of emotions work for you instead of against you. It is not just negative emotions that are contagious. Positive emotions such as excitement and joy are contagious as well. So ask yourself, "What emotional states do I want to propagate across my organization? What emotional climate do I want to create?" Using the contagiousness of emotions in this way, you can amplify your influence and your power.

> **POWER TALK (to self)**
>
> - "What emotions do I want to demonstrate and spread across my organization?"
> - "What is the emotional climate I want to create?"

One business leader I encountered specializes in "turnaround" situations—he goes into struggling organizations to reverse their business fortunes. "My biggest challenge in these contexts," he explained to me, "is changing the mood of the organization. When I arrive on the scene, it's as if there's a giant force trying to suck me into a vortex of helplessness and angry despair. My positivity and optimism have to be strong enough to outshine all that dark stuff. I have to pull everyone out of the hole they're in so that we can begin to make things happen."

While you manage the emotions you are transmitting, also be aware of what you are receiving. Especially be aware that sometimes, the contagiousness of emotions is not simply passive. Rather, people at times will *want* you to feel what they are feeling. If they are happy, they will want you to feel happy as well. And if they are unhappy, they will want you to feel this too. Your colleagues may not be aware they are doing this, but the mechanism is operating regardless. It is common and natural between people. So if you are not careful, you can be swept up in somebody else's negative emotions.

For example, a fearful colleague may want others around her, including you, to be fearful, too. Then she will feel less alone in her fear because you are fearful with her. This is why rumors of layoffs and other

Another way negative emotions spread is that people will tend to talk with you the same way they "talk" to themselves. So if they give themselves fear-inducing messages, they will likely give similar messages to you. If their self-talk tends to make them feel inadequate, they will likely create the same impact on you. Negative self-talk is very common. If you carefully manage your own, your communications with others will likely be more positive.

dreaded events spread so quickly within organizations. The fear of such things feels more tolerable when it is shared with others.

Similarly, a family member may pick a fight with you because he wants you to feel the anger he is feeling. If you are calm and unperturbed, that may be vexing for him. He will feel less alone in his anger—and thereby actually comforted—once he has pulled you down to his emotional level.

In more extreme cases, people don't try to simply share their negative states with you. Rather, they want to entirely unload them on you. They want you to take on all that they are feeling so they don't have to feel any of it. This is a very harmful psychological mechanism, and typically, it is done without awareness. For example, a colleague struggling with feelings of inadequacy may, in subtle ways, put you down. He is secretly hoping you will feel inadequate so that he won't have to. It is as if he could point his finger at you, saying, "She's the one who lacks self-confidence, not I." This is more common than you likely realize.

So when you start feeling negatively in the presence of a colleague, ask yourself, "Might I be feeling what *he's* feeling?" Know that you need not take on his emotions or anyone else's. In their struggles and distress, people sometimes want to pull you down into their negative states. Their emotions may feel too difficult to bear alone. Graciously resist their pull. You can be most helpful and best serve as a leader when you hold your power.

KEY POINTS TO REMEMBER

- Emotions commonly spread between people and across organizations.

- Sometimes, the propagation of negative emotions is not intended and is purely a result of their contagious nature.

- At other times, people will want you to feel their fear, anger, or feelings of inadequacy. They will feel better seeing that you share their emotions or even take them on entirely.

- So be alert to hold your power and not get "infected" by others' emotions or pulled into them. Also be careful that you do not inadvertently propagate negative emotions yourself. Instead, propagate positive ones by your presence and your example.

ACTIONS TO ENHANCE YOUR POWER

- Take ten minutes to reflect on how you are being impacted by other people's negative states. Is there anyone in whose presence you tend to get irritated? Or anxious? Or insecure? Might you be absorbing what they are feeling? Might they even *want* you to feel this way? Based on your answers, identify those situations in which you most need to be careful to maintain your emotional equilibrium. The following chapters will provide you more detailed instructions for doing so.

- Given that positive emotions are contagious just like negative ones, identify the emotions you want to transmit to other people. Consider creating a brief list of three emotions—such as enthusiasm, compassion, and caring—that you will regularly "radiate" so that others can absorb them. You may want to post this list in a place where you can regularly see it and be reminded of the impact you wish to have.

3

TRANSFORM YOUR FEAR
INTO COURAGE

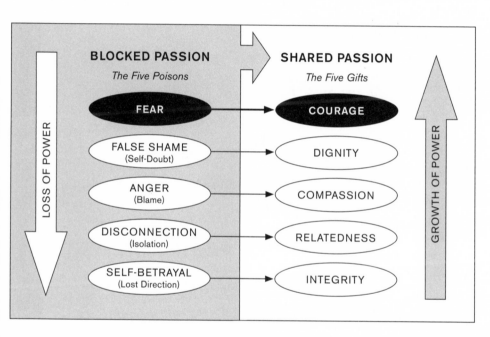

The Five Gifts Roadmap

NAME YOUR FEAR SO THAT YOU CAN TRANSFORM IT

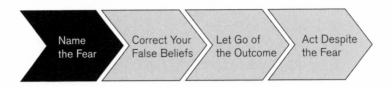

Name the Fear | Correct Your False Beliefs | Let Go of the Outcome | Act Despite the Fear

Your fear is to be expected, especially if you are leading others into an unknown future. You may not want to see the fear within you and it will often be in hiding. Suspect it is present, though, when the circumstances invite you to move forward, yet you are not taking action. Behind your rationales, you may find it is not logic but your fear that is talking. Be especially vigilant when your fear manifests as concerns that others may harm you or that you are in danger of failing. This is when your fear can seem most convincing—and when it is actually most harmful. As you discover your fear in its various disguises, name it so that it does not control you. And do so with compassion and self-acceptance. Identifying and transforming your fear is difficult enough without having to endure self-criticism.

If you look closely, you will find you feel fear often. This is only natural, especially if you are a leader. Your task as a person, and all the more so as a leader, is to push into the unknown future and make things happen. You are at the forefront, continuously moving into unfamiliar territory fraught with danger. The uncertainty you encounter will naturally generate fear within you.

Your fear may tempt you to stop moving and rest in the status quo. But fear is usually a poor mirror of reality. It is a poor guide for you. When you allow yourself to be guided by your fear, you are depleting your power.

Fear can appear in many forms, such as worry, nervousness, anxiety, and even dread. Frequently, though, your fear is operating quietly in the background. It is often there, influencing and even controlling you, with you barely even noticing it. And if you are like most leaders, you may not like your fear and may not want to see it. But if you are not aware of your fear and do not name it, you are more vulnerable to getting ensnared by it. Be diligent, then, in looking out for this danger to you.

For example, notice how you respond to change in your work and in your personal life as well. When big shifts in your workplace are necessary, do you always embrace the opportunities they present? Or are you sometimes a bit tentative and even, in subtle and silent ways, fearfully resistant? How about when your industry or field—or indeed the whole world—is changing at lightning speed around you? Do you run up and embrace the new realities? Or do you hesitate and even shrink back? And when your intimate partner states a desire for a new direction, do you open up and explore the possibilities? Or do you close down and let your fear take you over?

Observe the areas of your life where you are grasping too tightly. Are you not letting go of your current professional role—or your business, or a relationship or certain aspects of your identity—even though it no longer serves you and, in fact, harms you? Gripping what you have now, no matter how much it torments you, may feel safer than confronting your fears of the unknown future.

- "Is that my fear talking?"
- "Is my fear controlling me?"
- "How is my fear harming me?"

These are difficult questions to consider. But without asking them, you may drift along unaware that your fear is governing you and blocking your passion. Seeing how your fear operates will make you more powerful.

In looking within, be aware that fear often does not show itself plainly. Instead, it may masquerade as something rational. For example, a domineering CEO may say, "The timing isn't yet right for delegating my authority." And the leader moving too slowly and fearfully in making a decision may say, "I really need time to collect more information."

One of my clients was not taking the steps necessary for embarking on a major expansion of his business. Yet, his advisors were insisting he now had a key window of opportunity to do so. "I agree it's the right thing to do, but these things take time," he told me. "Could any of your emotions be hindering your progress?" I asked. "No," he abruptly replied. "At least for the past 30 years, I've never let *any* fears or worries or anything like that ever stop me from doing anything." But the next time I saw him, he reported to me a very interesting dream.

"I was standing on a very slippery rock on a cliff high above the ocean and there were these big, jagged rocks in the water below. People were expecting me to jump into the water. It was supposed to be no big deal."

"Could your dream relate to how you feel about expanding your business?" I asked. "Oh, I know it relates," he replied. "I've been waking up the past three mornings with enormous anxiety." Once he saw his fear, though, he could start addressing it directly.

Check to see if you might also be closing your eyes to your fears and deceiving yourself. When you hear yourself state rationales that keep you from moving forward, ask, "Is that my fear talking?" Bring your fear out of hiding and remove its disguise. Name it and see it for what it is. Then you can challenge it directly and stop it from impeding your progress.

Beware of two especially destructive forms of fear. Your awareness will protect you from them.

One such fear is an unfounded worry that certain people may harm you and, perhaps, even wish to do so. You may think you hardly have such fears. But look carefully, as they are common and often subtle. Perhaps you fear certain colleagues, or certain residents of your city. Perhaps you fear the members of a certain ethnic group or the people that make up a particular nation. To get clearer about whom you fear, simply ask yourself, "Whom do I not trust? Whom am I not open to?"

Be careful about buying into these fears too readily. If you act on them rather than transforming them, you will be shutting out potential friends and allies. Rather than seeing people for who they truly are, you will be erecting barriers against them. You will be generating mistrust and, likely, much conflict.

Although your fear of others may not be justified at the outset, it will likely be self-fulfilling once you put it into action. During an economic downturn, the general managers of two divisions within a company were asked to allocate between themselves a significant number of layoffs. As many jobs were at stake, the atmosphere was charged with strong emotions. The allocations were to be based on each division's business prospects, yet one of the general managers withheld information—arguably vital—from the other. She later explained to me why she had done so. "Frankly, I don't trust him," she said. "He would have misused that data to try to force my business to take on more than our fair share of the cutbacks."

After the layoffs were already agreed to and announced, the withheld information surfaced. Despite the general manager's insistence that the data was "not very relevant," her counterpart was furious and attacked her. "You see?" she told me. "He is dangerous and vindictive." "But do you see," I asked her, "how he might feel misled by you?" It was painful for her to look, but she saw that this was an enemy she herself had created.

Observe carefully to see if you, too, are creating your enemies. Ask, "Am I creating the very adversaries that frighten and torment me?" These enemies are like characters in a play of your own writing.

- "Do I have to have these enemies—or did I create them?"
- "Am I really seeing this person—or am I just seeing my fear?"
- "Did my fear create this conflict I'm in?"

DEEPER WISDOM

When you close off to people due to your fear, this can elicit a number of strong emotional reactions in them, depending on their personalities. Some people will feel rejected and hurt. Some will feel angry and even wrathful. Others may fear you are about to harm them. Any of these emotional reactions can trigger defensive maneuvers and even attacks against you. Acting on your fear, therefore, may be more dangerous to you than whatever you initially feared.

Prejudices and even wars arise in this way. When you fear a group of people, be mindful of how they may be experiencing your reactions. When you avoid them and build your fences and shields, you are signaling you do not like them and fear them. Seeing this, they will suspect you are inclined toward harming them. Then they will fear you too. Naturally, they will take countermeasures, and soon you could find yourself in a terrible conflict.

Likely, you have observed some conflicts in your workplace—or in your family. Have you noticed how each side gets so caught up in their fears that it is hard for them to see the humanity and vulnerability of the other people? As each person acts on his fears to protect himself, the others feel harmed and more threatened and therefore take their own self-protective action. This leads to yet more fear and more reaction. It is a downward spiral that is equally co-created.

Conflicts and wars such as this are common. They grow out of irrational fears that ultimately seem justified. Be careful or you may wage such wars yourself. So when you find yourself in a conflict, ask, "Is my fear governing my actions? Is there a more rational and powerful way of proceeding?"

The second type of highly destructive fear to be alert for is not fear of others, but rather fear of yourself. Specifically, it is the fear that you lack the necessary abilities and will fail. This fear of failure is extremely common in leaders. Consider carefully if it may be present and operating within you.

As is true for many leaders, this fear may have once been a driving force in your success. Fearing failure, you may have worked inordinately hard to avoid it. Ultimately, though, acting on this fear will limit you. It will cause you to expend your energies inefficiently and it will drain your passion. As you toil under the dark cloud of fear, your work may become drudgery, lacking creativity and inspiration.

The fear of failure causes its greatest harm in stopping people from taking on larger challenges and pursuing what they most desire. Ask yourself if this is happening in your own life, too. Are you, like many people, and like many leaders, remaining in a role that is not satisfying for you? Have you stopped growing? Look carefully to see if you are afraid to pursue what you really want lest you fail. Look to see if you are playing it safe and starving your passion.

> **POWER TALK (to self)**
>
> - "Is my fear keeping me in a role or situation that is no longer working for me?"
> - "Is my fear keeping me from growing?"

In those instances where you cannot see your fear of failure directly, you can still infer it. Simply observe where your forward movement has stalled despite your having the means to continue. Quite possibly, it is your fear that is blocking you. So shine a light on the fear and examine it rather than allowing it to govern you surreptitiously. Then you can deliberately make a decision about your forward progress that best serves you.

As you look to see how fear may be operating within you in these various ways, remember to accept yourself with compassion and kindness. Dealing with your fear is difficult enough without having to endure self-criticism and shame for it. When you are willing to accept your fear, you will also be willing to acknowledge it when it arises within you. And that enables you to address it and, ultimately, to transform it.

KEY POINTS TO REMEMBER

- As a leader, you regularly encounter the uncertainty of the future and move into it. Naturally, you will feel fear along the way. When you identify the fear within you and name it, you will much less likely get ensnared by it. Naming your fear makes you more powerful.

- Often, your fear will not be plainly visible to you. It may operate quietly in the background, just on the edge of your awareness. And it will frequently masquerade as rationales to stop you from your forward progress.

- An especially destructive form of fear is fearing harm from certain people. If you harbor such fear without carefully examining it, you may unnecessarily erect barriers against others and generate conflict.

- Another highly destructive form of fear is fearing that you lack the requisite ability and will therefore fail. If you irrationally have this fear and act on it, you may be holding yourself back from taking on larger challenges and doing what you most desire.

- As you see your fear and name it, be compassionate with yourself. Your kind self-acceptance, rather than harsh self-criticism, will facilitate your identification of your fears and their transformation.

ACTIONS TO ENHANCE YOUR POWER

- Sit down in a quiet place and ask yourself, "What do I want to be doing in my professional life—and my personal life—that I'm not doing?" Also ask, "What challenges am I not addressing?" Make a list of these items. Consider whether it is fear that has been holding you back. If fear has been the determining force, consider to what extent you want to continue being guided by it.

- Set aside an additional time of quiet for identifying the people you fear may harm you. Don't too quickly accept an initial response of "No one." Look more closely. Then ask yourself, "How do I know these fears are valid?" Also examine whether you have acted on any of these fears. Ask yourself, "To what extent have I created these very enemies that I'm now fearing?"

IDENTIFY AND CORRECT THE
FALSE BELIEFS DRIVING YOUR FEAR

Once you become aware of fear arising within you, insistently question the beliefs that support it. You may notice that you often resist doing so. That is your fear whispering to you, "Listen to me and you will be safer." But when you expose your fear to the light, you will often see it is actually putting you in danger. It is closing you off to the people who will help you correct your distorted beliefs about them. And it is cutting you off from knowing and experiencing your true capacities. By continuously challenging the beliefs that feed your fear, you will undo much of it and reduce the rest to appropriate caution.

Your fear typically grows out of distorted beliefs that purport to warn and even protect you. But the pictures they paint of your powerlessness are likely not true. When you succumb to these fears and act on them, you are not quite operating in reality. Rather, you are in a separate and unhappy world of your own making. That is a danger to you. Consider safeguarding yourself from such an outcome by challenging the beliefs upon which your fears are built. In doing this regularly, you will better hold your power.

For example, when you fear that a particular person will harm you, examine your beliefs about him or her carefully. Using the PEA (Perception–Emotion–Action) chains I described in Chapter 1, identify the perceptions or beliefs driving your emotion. By identifying the actions you are taking in response to your fear, you can assess its cost to you, too.

You may notice, though, a resistance to examining your beliefs. You may feel certain your fear is justified. But the greater danger to you may not be what you fear, but acting on your fear and generating more mistrust and conflict.

Two executives at the same company harmed each other in this manner. One was fearful the other was trying to take over some of her responsibilities. And the other was convinced that his colleague was speaking poorly about him and tarnishing his reputation. Neither person had ever openly examined their fears because they were also fearful of having a candid discussion with each other. Both leaders were assertive and forceful, yet under the surface, it was their unchallenged fears that were controlling them. Therefore, the hardness and bitterness between them was very apparent.

To expose their fears, I facilitated a conversation with the two of them. At the outset of the meeting, they were stiff and unsmiling, but as they gradually revealed the relevant facts about themselves and their conduct, it became clear how dramatically distorted were their views of each other. Not only did their fears progressively diminish over the course of the meeting, but the atmosphere in the room also grew markedly lighter. After two hours of dialogue, I noticed that the male executive's face was now so emptied of tension that he looked like an entirely different person.

"You look different now," I commented. "I feel different," he replied. And then he looked to his colleague and said with a smile, "She looks different, too." They both laughed. I thought to myself, "Who would have guessed this could happen?"

When you fear people, you close off to them. You prevent yourself from learning the truth that would undo your fear. Our world is filled with leaders whose vision is blocked in these ways. How about you? Are you holding destructive fears that would soon dissolve if only you exposed them to scrutiny? Are you resisting doing so? Perhaps you feel your fears are protecting you and so you want to hold on to them. But that only keeps you locked inside of them.

When you fear that you will not perform well enough, question your perceptions here, too, so that your fear does not govern you. Question your beliefs about your abilities or that you are not doing enough and must work harder. Perhaps the greater danger for you is being chased by your fear and not being in your power. I hardly ever see an executive who is not working hard enough. But I see many executives preoccupied with their fears and thereby undermining their confidence and passion.

When I gave my first workshop inside a large organization many years ago, I was fearful I would not perform well and that the content I was teaching would not be sufficient, either. Instead of questioning my fears, I acted on them. I took on the very arduous task of memorizing nearly every word I'd say over the entire two-day period. But at the end of the program, as we said our good-byes, I was so moved that I departed from my script. On the edge of tears, I spoke from my heart. I told the participants how much the workshop had meant to me on a personal level.

DEEPER WISDOM

People also resist examining their fears because they are concerned they may actually find them to be invalid. Then they will have to feel all the loss and pain, and perhaps embarrassment and shame as well, of having unnecessarily limited themselves for so long. Rather than enduring those feelings, it may seem more comfortable to adhere to the old way of seeing things. Of course, this only creates more loss and pain.

I was surprised to learn from the participants' feedback afterward that this was one of their favorite moments. They had wanted me to be more fluid and spontaneous with them. It dawned on me that by enacting my fears about my performance, I had actually impaired it and, apart from my farewell at the end, had choked off much of my passion.

Your fears about your own performance can spill over into fearing your direct reports' performance—and even that of your children—as well. Be mindful of how this impacts them. Just as your fears about yourself can undermine your own confidence, your fears about others' performance can undermine theirs.

A very exacting manager complained to me that he wanted to delegate more of his responsibilities, but he feared his team members would not perform them properly. He imagined all kinds of possible negative outcomes. "Part of the problem," he said, "is they lack self-confidence." I asked him, "Could your worries about your people and your decision, therefore, to not delegate much to them be a cause of their poor confidence?" He looked at me quizzically and then said, "That's an interesting perspective."

After he started to experiment with greater delegation and we observed the results, he raised a different topic. He shared with me his anxieties about his son's social awkwardness. He said, "I'm beginning to see the effect my worries have had on my team. Could it be I've been having a similar effect on my children?"

So when you notice your fear, ask yourself, "Are my beliefs actually correct? How do I know they are true?" Put your fears on trial and examine the evidence pro and con. You do not need to believe what your fears are telling you. Your fear is like an emotional colleague bursting into your office, demanding your immediate attention. But you can hold your power in the face of this intrusion.

You may believe that when you act based on your fear, you are safer. But if you examine the facts, you will likely see that acting on your fear typically undermines your power and creates more danger. Your fear will frequently counsel you to slow down or stop. Sometimes this may be appropriate. But being a powerful leader often requires you to decisively move forward. People want to see and feel your strength and boldness, as well as your wisdom, in the face of

POWER TALK (to self)

- "Are my beliefs actually correct?"
- "How do I know they are true?"
- "I don't need to believe what my fear is telling me."

your fear. So look out for your fear, and when it arises, challenge the beliefs that support it.

summary

KEY POINTS TO REMEMBER

- Your fear purports to protect you, but it is often based on beliefs that are not true. Therefore, it is crucial that you regularly identify and challenge those beliefs.

- If you let it, your fear will prevent you from openly speaking with the people you believe may harm you. But if you have these conversations despite your fear, you will find it typically shrinks or even disappears.

- If you are fearful about your own abilities, you will tend to have similar fears about the people you manage as well. But upon examination, you may find that it is actually your fears about your direct reports that undermine their confidence and therefore their performance.

- Overall, as you examine the beliefs underlying your fears, you will likely find that the greatest danger to you is not what you thought, but is acting on your fears and thereby damaging your relationships and blocking your passion.

ACTIONS TO ENHANCE YOUR POWER

- In the first exercise in the prior section, you identified the challenges you are avoiding. For each of those challenges, now identify the beliefs that are holding you back. Next, ask yourself, "How do I know these beliefs are true?" List the evidence supporting each belief and the evidence tending to refute it as well. Then ask yourself, "Have I actually proved this belief to be true?" As you decide whether to continue accepting these beliefs, also consider the harm they cause you.

- In the second exercise in the prior section, you identified the people you fear may harm you. Now identify the beliefs supporting these fears as well. List the evidence regarding each belief, pro and con. Also consider how these beliefs negatively affect you and others. Then ask yourself, "Do I want to continue accepting these beliefs as true?"

NEUTRALIZE YOUR FEAR
BY LETTING GO OF THE OUTCOME

Your fear is limited to what may happen in the future. It cannot affect you when you focus your efforts on the immediate present. So when your fear arises, see what you can do in that moment rather than depleting your energies on what is beyond your control in the unknowable future. You can further lessen your fear by focusing on the bigger picture. Keep in mind a vision of the leader you intend to be and the contributions you intend to make to others. Unlike future events external to you, these are within your control and therefore within the realm of your power.

To the extent you feel an event beyond your control *must* or *must not* happen, you will feel fear about that very thing. In that way, you will be blocking your passion and your power. Like it or not, you generally cannot control the future. But you can control how you show up as a person and as a leader. When you do so diligently, moment by moment, then you will be back in the realm of your power. The future is the domain of your fear and the present is the domain of your power.

So when fear arises within you, see what you can do in the immediate present to be effective and influence the future. Ask yourself, "What can I do *right now* to be most powerful?" And once you've done everything you can to effect the result, release the rest. If you grip too tightly to what must or might happen, then fear will emerge and deplete you. By letting go of the result, you will actually have greater passion.

Executives sometimes tell me, "Dean, this is all well and good, but I can't let go of the outcome. I *have* to make my numbers." You, too, may hold to outcomes that "have to" happen. They may be in your work life and in your family life too. But if you worry and fret about the future beyond what you can do in the present, you are only increasing your sense of powerlessness. This will impact how you show up as a leader. The people around you will respond accordingly.

A young and driven executive I encountered had habitually focused on very high goals for himself that, time and again, he was actually able to achieve. Yet, when his industry went into a downturn, his ambitious goals grew increasingly out of reach. He did not adjust his goals accordingly; rather, his fear of failure drove him into a near-frenzy of effort. This was not the approach he needed.

"The wheels are beginning to come off the cart," his CEO confided in me, "and that doesn't inspire my confidence. Can he still bear down hard but be unfazed by what comes at him—including results that may be disappointing? Could he have such a maturity that almost nothing throws him off track? He's got to change course because right now, his power is slipping."

Your goals, however, are still important. They can activate your energies and inspire you and others. They can constellate the efforts of you and your colleagues. But be aware when your goals activate your fears more than your energies. Ask yourself, "Is my goal energizing me or is it oppressing me?" Then deal with the goal accordingly.

> **POWER TALK (to self)**
>
> - "Is my goal energizing me—or is it just activating my fear and oppressing me?"
>
> - "What is the most powerful thing I can do right now?"

Instead of being so attached to the unpredictable outcomes of your efforts, it is often better to be guided by something you can fully control. Consider, then, being guided by the greater reality of who you intend to be as a human being and as a leader. Create a vision of how you will conduct yourself—independent of circumstances and outcomes. If you commit to this vision and hold to it, that will buffer you against your fears and any disappointing results. Rather than being pushed and pulled by the vagaries of the moment and responding with fear, you will be anchored in something more solid and under your control.

Consider expanding your perspective even further. What you fear is typically not that important in light of your life's bigger picture. Think back to your fears of 10 or 20 years ago. How important are they now? To what extent can you even remember them? Or imagine looking back on your life near its end. In that context, will the outcomes you now fret about be so important? Perhaps what will then appear as most significant is how you acted in your life.

A man I came to know had fought pitched battles for the control of several organizations. He had a reputation as a fierce boardroom warrior, and legend had it that once, long ago, he had even thrown a typewriter at a colleague. I found him one day in his garden, among many ripe, plump tomatoes hanging from their vines. He was retired now, and his sunburned face was deeply wrinkled.

"Now I see," he said, peering from under the rim of his tattered straw hat, "how much I was driven by fear, by the fear of losing. And this may sound strange, but somehow, growing these tomatoes—planting the seeds, watering them, watching them come up, and then giving them away to my children and my grandchildren and my neighbors—feels a lot more important to me than all those struggles earlier in my life. All that stuff back then, it seemed very significant, but now I have a different perspective."

So when you notice yourself caught up in fears about the outcomes of your efforts, ask yourself, "But what is the bigger picture?" Even ask, "What is my life *really* about?" And if you are a business leader, also ask, "What is my leadership really about? Is it more than growing the business and making it more successful?" Perhaps your leadership also concerns something deeper. For example, it may be about the contributions you can make to others and the growth you and they can experience together.

This type of inquiry will not make you less effective as a leader. Rather, it will make you more so. Your concern about the success of your efforts, instead of being fearful and anxious, will be more balanced and solid. You may even reach a point where you see your business results primarily as measures of your growth and your contributions as a leader. Then you can be more focused on contributing—to your colleagues, customers, constituencies, and investors—and less distracted by outcomes you cannot control. Focusing your efforts in this way will render you more powerful.

> **POWER TALK (to self)**
>
> - "How do I intend to conduct myself as a person and as a leader?"
> - "What do I want to give to my organization and to my people?"

Question, then, what else you can focus on beyond narrowly defined results. Consider what else is important in your leadership. I once worked with a very popular and effective leader at a specialty food retailer. She confided in me, "Dean, I don't care so much about the bean dip. What I really care about is the people." She reflected for a moment and added, "This is what my leadership is really about."

A father I know was terribly worried about his son's academic performance and often pointedly spoke to him about the issue. The boy's grades did not improve as a result. But he did get as worried as his father and eventually developed medical problems, which progressively grew more serious. Finally, a physician told the father, "If you don't ease up on your son, you're going to kill him."

"I was shocked," the father told me. "I realized I had to let go of my obsession with his grades. Now, I just focus on two things with my son: What type of father do I want to be? And what do I want to give to him?" They are now both doing much better.

How about you? Are you bearing down too hard and just intensifying fear in yourself and in others? You are the father, or the mother, of your team or organization—and of your projects and special endeavors. You cannot entirely control how they grow up. But you can control how you show up and the contributions you make to those around you.

summary

KEY POINTS TO REMEMBER

- Your fear will naturally be activated when you feel some event *must* or *must not* happen in the future, especially if that event is not under your control. Fear is an emotion about the *future*.

- You can therefore neutralize your fear when you let go of things having to happen in a certain way and, instead, focus on what you can do in the present moment. And once you've done everything you can to effect the result, release the rest. The future is the domain of your fear, and the present is the domain of your power.

- You can also lessen your fear about outcomes beyond your control by focusing on the bigger picture. For example, focus on how you intend to conduct yourself as a leader. And focus on the contributions you intend to make to your colleagues. These are within your control and therefore attending to them will enhance your sense of your power.

ACTIONS TO ENHANCE YOUR POWER

- Ask yourself, "What am I afraid will or will not happen?" For each fear you identify, see if you can find a bigger-picture perspective that is helpful. For example, imagine viewing the fear at the end of your life. Will it be so important then? Also ask, "Can my focus be more on my own actions that I can control rather than on the outcomes that I cannot?" Then observe the effect these approaches have on your fears.

ACT RESOLUTELY DESPITE YOUR FEAR
TO COMPLETE ITS TRANSFORMATION

| Name the Fear | Correct Your False Beliefs | Let Go of the Outcome | Act Despite the Fear |

To be most powerful in the face of your fear, do the very things it tells you not to. In so acting, you will weaken and diminish your fear, transforming it into courage. And as you move forward, you will likely get confirmation that your fearful beliefs have not been true. Act wisely, though, first verifying that your fear is probably invalid. Also act incrementally, step by step, if you sense your fear will otherwise stop you. Each small step you take and acknowledge to yourself will embolden you to take the next. Keep moving forward into your fear, less concerned about outcomes and more focused on the expansion of your freedom and your power. To assist you in your progress, welcome your fear as a signal that you're about to grow further.

Your most powerful response to fear is to proceed in the direction contrary to where it guides you. This transforms your fear into courage. Likely, you cannot stop your fear from arising. But you can continuously transform it by taking action despite what it tells you.

So once you become aware of fear within, first examine it to confirm it's likely invalid. Assuming that's the case, let go of the outcome and then take action. In doing so, you will enhance your power. Every time you heed your fear, you feed it and it will grow larger. And every time you act courageously, you starve it and it becomes smaller.

Do you fear doing something new and stepping into a greater expression of your power? How are you responding to that fear? When you don't proceed in the face of it, you lose the opportunity to see it's unfounded. Taking action despite your fear exposes the false beliefs that support it. Yet, as you move forward into your fear, initially it will get louder. View your discomfort as a welcome sign that you are now headed in the right direction.

Your fear is standing at the boundaries of your limiting self-enclosures. It is signaling to you that you now have an opportunity to grow and move into a greater self-expression. So when you feel fear, step through it and take action. Then watch and see how this expands your capacities and your power. If, on the other hand, you are not feeling fear, this may be telling you that you are playing it safe, not testing your limits and growing past them.

I once mentored a young boy who, when he was two years old, was held outside a third-story window by his drug-addicted mother. She was threatening to drop him. Understandably, he now had a fear of heights. But there was something powerful within him that was driven to conquer his fear. And so when we would go to the playground together, he would jump off the play structure at progressively greater heights while I stood below and caught him. One day, while my back was turned, he scrambled to the very top of the ten-foot structure and stood on top of it.

"Dean!" he shrieked, "Catch me!" I spun around to see a little boy flying through the air, coming right at me. I reached out and caught him. He never jumped from the structure again. He had healed his fear.

To avoid what frightens you is natural. But to maximize your growth and your power, seek out experiences that actually activate your fear. Then, gently yet persistently, push into it. Assess your efforts not so much by the results, but by how far back you have moved the boundaries of your fear and expanded your freedom.

POWER TALK (to self)

- "Am I feeding my fear now? Or am I starving it?"
- "What can I do in this moment that counters my fear?"

You need not insist of yourself that you tackle the worst of your fears immediately. That may make your fear intolerable. Instead, consider acting incrementally, taking one small step after the other. The steps can be as tiny as you want them to be. The crucial factor is that you are taking them and moving forward. Each step will embolden you to take the next. Compassionately en*courage* yourself at every step along the way. By doing so, you give yourself the *courage* to move forward. Then, after each step you take, acknowledge yourself for your boldness.

Years ago, I dreamed of building an independent consulting practice but was terrified I'd fail. So I wasn't taking any action at all. Finally, I realized I could perform one small action—I bought a book that showed me how to use a graphics software program. I acknowledged myself for this. "Good," I said, "now I'm one step closer to realizing my goal." Then I read some of the book. Then I explored the graphics program a bit. Then, as I was learning it, I created the Four Powers Pyramid you saw in Chapter 1. Within one year, I was teaching workshops globally at large corporations.

At every step along the way, I acknowledged myself for my progress. Instead, I could have berated myself for not moving faster. I could have told myself, as I often have, "You're not doing enough!" Perhaps you have that unhelpful habit, too. If I had defaulted to it in this case, it might have shut down my efforts. I needed to just take one step after the other.

Many people alternately inspire and terrify themselves with plans for great achievements. And then they typically don't move forward. Are you one of those people, too? Instead of telling yourself, "I have to perform this great feat," simply identify the next small step you *can* and *will* take. And then take it. And then the next, and so on. If you're not taking your next step, that means you've made it too large and are too frightened to take action. Back off a bit and choose something smaller. And then move forward.

Be careful, though, that the actions you take counter to your fears truly enhance your growth rather than harm you. If, for example, you fear wrathful bosses—or wrathful spouses—and keep choosing them, this is not necessarily benefiting you. When people repeatedly run into the face of their fears without self-compassion and self-awareness, this is called *counterphobic behavior*. Such conduct, when you engage in it, only harms you. Instead, be kind with yourself and continuously mindful. Then you can proceed skillfully in transforming your fears and growing your power.

Imagine no longer letting fear stop you from speaking your truth and living your passion. Imagine all that you could make happen. When you transform your fear into courage, you will enjoy such an expansion of your power.

DEEPER WISDOM

Counterphobic behavior is a form of *compensation*—people doing and appearing the opposite of what they actually feel inside. For example, someone acts aggressively confident, but actually feels very inadequate deep within. A problem with compensation is that the underlying feelings remain and still drive the person's behavior. Another problem is that compensation often has the effect of intimidating others. Consider, then, whether you may be using this mechanism. And if you see others who seem extreme on any dimension, suspect that they may be using it as well. Under the surface, they may be feeling just the opposite of what they are showing.

KEY POINTS TO REMEMBER

- Your most powerful tool for transforming your fear is acting contrary to what it tells you. Your acting in this way is courage.

- If you don't proceed in the face of your fear, you will be deprived of the opportunity to see that the beliefs supporting it are invalid.

- Your fear will tend to get activated as you approach what you believe to be your limitations. View your fear as a signal that you are about to grow should you move forward. And if you are not feeling fear, this may be signaling that you are playing it safe and are stalled in your progress.

- To transform a fear, you need not tackle it all at once. Instead, you can challenge it incrementally, step by step. Each step, no matter how small, will embolden you to take the next. The important issue is not the size of the steps, but that you keep moving forward.

- In challenging your fear, proceed with self-compassion and self-awareness. Otherwise, you may act counterphobically, repeatedly pushing into the same fears in a way that harms you.

ACTIONS TO ENHANCE YOUR POWER

- Identify one fear that you will erode over the next one to three months by acting contrary to it. Write out a plan of action. It may involve fully challenging your fear all at once and doing so repeatedly. Or the better course may be proceeding one small step at a time. Either way, be sure to acknowledge yourself for each action you take contrary to your fear. It's best if you do so in writing. Each acknowledgment will be emotional fuel for the next action you take. After you have made sufficient progress with one fear, start addressing another. At all times, have at least one fear that you are actively encountering and diminishing. This will ensure that you are continuously growing your power.

4

TRANSFORM YOUR
FALSE SHAME INTO DIGNITY

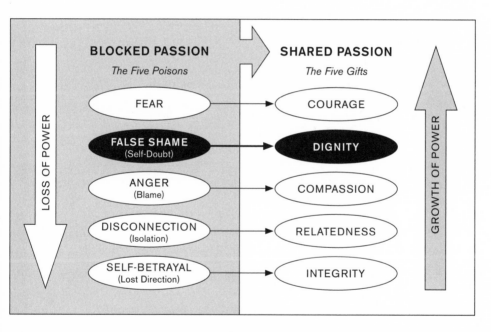

The Five Gifts Roadmap

RECOGNIZE YOUR FALSE SHAME
IN ITS MANY GUISES

| Recognize the False Shame | > | Correct Distorted Beliefs | > | Deepen Your Self-Acceptance | > | Develop Your Humility | > | Take Action |

If you look inside of yourself and look closely, you will likely find feelings of self-doubt and inadequacy. Do not be surprised, for such feelings are very common, including in leaders. These emotions are called false shame because you would never feel badly about yourself if you could see yourself clearly. As you come to recognize your false shame in its various guises, you will see how it limits you and blocks your passion. It may manifest as fears of failure or rejection. Or it may manifest as a fear of learning about yourself and how others perceive you. Then you may deprive yourself of information crucial to you. To counter your feelings of inadequacy, you may also try too hard to be right or nearly perfect, or you may compete needlessly. This will only strengthen your self-doubt and turn others against you. It may be painful to see your false shame, but that's the first step in its transformation.

Feelings of inadequacy are very common, including among leaders. If you look inside, you will likely find them present within you too. They may arise as feelings of being unworthy or "insecure." You may feel a lack of self-confidence or a bothersome self-doubt. You may feel like an "impostor" and, in comparison to others, find yourself lacking. As you identify these emotions, observe how much they may be holding you back and blocking your power. Your self-awareness is the first step in their transformation.

I call these emotions in their different variations *false shame*. Shame is the emotion that tells you, "I'm not good enough; I'm unworthy." The shame is false because it is irrational and unwarranted. If you could only see yourself clearly and fully, and with compassion, you would never feel any shame. Instead, you would be touched by the sincerity and magnitude of your efforts. You would be moved by your inherent goodness and value. Even reading the prior sentence or two may activate your false shame. You may

find yourself saying, "That's not true!" That's your false shame talking. It's a dense filter that grossly distorts your self-perception. It is very unfair to you.

You need not conclusively decide at this moment which perceptions of you are accurate. In the sections that follow, I will give you tools and more information for doing so. For now, simply consider how active your false shame is and how much it may be harming you. When I work with leaders, I pull out the Five Gifts Roadmap and I ask them, "Where are you?" The great majority of them point to "False Shame" and say, "Right here." Does that describe you, too? Open to seeing these feelings that are operating inside of you. Then you can start freeing yourself from them.

False shame often appears as a variety of fears. In fact, fear and false shame often go together. For example, when you fear failing in a job or in a challenge, your fear is likely intensified by your feeling unworthy. When you transform your false shame, much of your fear of failure will fade away, too.

If you fear rejection, that, too, is mostly driven by your false shame. So when you fear approaching a person and asking for an opportunity, when you fear "asking for the sale," and when you fear telling others what you most deeply want to give and what you desire, this is really your unwarranted feelings of unworthiness impeding you. When you know your own true worth and *feel* it, you will not be so afraid of how people may respond to you. You will know they cannot affect how you experience your own value.

One of the most harmful expressions of false shame is the fear of seeing yourself clearly. If you, like most people, have this fear, what you actually fear is the *false* shame you may feel when you observe yourself closely. But self-awareness is the foundation for your self-mastery and your power. If you don't see yourself accurately, you cannot change most effectively. And to modify how people respond to you, you need to know how they currently see you.

Yet, many leaders avoid this type of information. They are letting their false shame govern their actions. One CEO took it a step further. Just as he feared his own false shame, he also feared activating it in others. So he avoided getting clear and direct feedback, and he avoided giving it as well. When I attempted to give him feedback about this very point, he denied it was an issue. He insisted, "I'm *always* very open with my feedback." And then he signaled he wanted to change the topic.

Tragically, his direct reports were only learning of his unhappiness with them when he was already close to firing them. And then it was often too late.

Consider, then, if you are letting your false shame block your access to essential information about yourself, including how others see you. This is similar to not looking at your financial statements, or not looking in the mirror, for fear of what you may discover. To navigate in life and lead most effectively, you need this knowledge. Therefore, it is crucial to resolve the false shame that keeps you from it.

Instead of acting directly on your false shame, you may try to move in the opposite direction. In doing so, you may hope to counteract these feelings and "make up for" them. But if your self-doubt is still driving your actions, this is merely *compensation,* which I described in the prior chapter. Acting in this way does not lessen your false shame. Rather, it gets you more ensnared in it.

For example, do you sometimes need to be "right" and show others how knowledgeable you are? If so, perhaps you are trying to avoid feeling unworthy. Perhaps, even, you go further and neither seek nor use others' ideas, lest they prove to be better than your own. If you act in these ways to guard against your feelings of inadequacy, you are likely triggering those same feelings in others. They will therefore resent you and may take action against you to make you feel inadequate instead.

A university administrator I observed at a meeting appeared to automatically disagree with nearly everything his colleagues suggested. By the end of the session, they seemed dispirited and exasperated. In my private conversation with the administrator afterward, it became apparent that he was unaware of his pattern of behavior. He was especially surprised by my suggestion that, given his conduct, his peers were feeling devalued. "Really?" he asked. "But they all seem quite confident."

When I inquired about his own level of confidence among his colleagues, he acknowledged this was a bit of a challenge. "I secretly feel rather flawed," he confided. "Is it a secret," I asked, "that you even try to keep from yourself?" "Most of the time," he said quietly, as he leaned back in his chair and folded his arms across his chest.

Perhaps you use an alternative strategy and, like many people, try to do some tasks per-fectly, or nearly so, unaware you are seeking to buttress your own value. If this describes you, consider that you are likely doing more than is needed. Consider, then, the costs of this pat-tern to you. It may be draining your energies and diverting you from greater opportunities.

In fact, your excessively high standards may be protecting you from taking on greater tasks that can activate your false shame. For example, perhaps you are avoiding thinking more deeply about the direction in which your company needs to grow. Or perhaps you are avoiding where you personally need to de-velop. Because these tasks are not so discrete and clearly defined, be-cause they can't be done perfectly and checked off your list, they can naturally stir up your feelings of inadequacy. But the most important tasks are often like this. Avoiding them and indulging your perfection-ism with small tasks instead is likely harming you.

Personally, it is easier for me to work on perfecting the appearance of a document or presentation than to stare into the face of my great-est self-doubts and then take action. But I have noticed that the more I indulge this pattern, the more I feed my feelings of inadequacy. Perfec-tionism, I have come to see, is false mastery. It typically only provides a mastery of things that are not important. Consider instead working toward a mastery of your true power.

Your self-doubt may also emerge in the form of counterproductive competition. Executives compete with each other to get the most influ-ence and resources. Siblings compete about who will be most successful. And parents compete to see whose child is doing better. This competition is typically fueled by false shame. If you truly felt good about yourself and your value, what, if anything, would you really need to prove?

This does not mean you should eschew all competition. But be careful that when you do compete, it is not shame-based, but honors you and your opponents. View the competition as a noble contest that has, as its ultimate purpose, your and your colleagues' growth and evolution. This is the true meaning of "good sportsmanship." It is where the mere results of the contest are secondary to the humanity and dignity of the participants.

If you are engaging in shame-based competition instead, you are erecting walls between yourself and others. Likely, those around you are feeling intimidated, annoyed, and resentful. In these ways, you are harming your relationships and thereby blocking your power. Rather than depleting your energy in competition that does not serve you, consider instead transforming the false shame that propels it. Once you know your true worth, you will have no need to prove it to others.

> **POWER TALK (to self)**
>
> - "Is it false shame that makes me so competitive?"
> - "How else is my false shame controlling me?"
> - "How is it harming my relationships and blocking my power?"

Likely, you've already been told many times, "Be confident." That simple advisory probably does not help you. The question is *how* to transform your false shame so that you can indeed be confident. In the following sections, I will show you.

KEY POINTS TO REMEMBER

- Feelings of inadequacy, unworthiness, and self-doubt are very common in people, including in leaders. Therefore, they are likely present within you as well. These emotions undermine your relationships and obstruct your power.

- These feelings, called *false shame*, are irrational and unwarranted. The shame is false because if you could see yourself clearly, you would never feel any shame or feelings of inadequacy.

- Becoming aware of your false shame and the various ways it manifests within you gives you power over it and enables you to begin its transformation.

- False shame may appear within you as fears of failing or being rejected. And it may arise as a fear of learning about yourself and how others see you. That can cause you to avoid information crucial to being more effective.

- You may want to counter your feelings of inadequacy by trying to always be right or nearly perfect and by needlessly competing against others. Acting in these ways, though, will only strengthen your false shame and cause others to fear, resent, and avoid you.

ACTIONS TO ENHANCE YOUR POWER

- Review the descriptions of the different ways people directly and indirectly allow false shame to govern their actions. While reading, ask yourself, "How does false shame affect *my* conduct?" See if you can identify at least three habitual ways of acting that are fueled by your false shame. Then assess how each of these patterns may be harming your relationships and undermining your power. Determine which of these patterns you are ready to free yourself from now. The following sections will provide you the necessary tools and strategies.

CORRECT THE DISTORTED BELIEFS
FUELING YOUR FALSE SHAME

Recognize the False Shame › **Correct Distorted Beliefs** › Deepen Your Self-Acceptance › Develop Your Humility › Take Action

Negative and highly distorted beliefs about yourself are feeding your false shame. You may think your self-critical views push you to higher levels of achievement, but that's a false belief, too. Your self-criticism actually undermines your confidence and dangerously depletes you. No doubt you have your limitations, but your beliefs are likely magnifying them and thereby harming you. So when you notice your false shame emerging, clearly identify the underlying beliefs and directly challenge them. Review the evidence supporting the beliefs and the evidence opposing them as well. In doing so, you will likely find many of them to be grossly untrue. As you correct your beliefs about yourself, your false shame will shrink, thereby unblocking your passion and enhancing your power.

Your false shame emanates from beliefs about yourself that, typically, are grossly untrue. As you identify these beliefs and challenge them head-on, they will begin to release their hold on you. Then your false shame will fall away in equal degree.

Look carefully, then, to determine your beliefs that undermine your self-worth. For example, you may say, like a brilliant scientist-leader I knew, "I'm not that intelligent." Or despite your many obvious achievements, you may say, "I haven't done much at all." Deep inside, you may even be saying, "Really, I'm a failure." In my work with successful leaders, I often hear them make these self-critical remarks and many more. Their beliefs are utterly irrational and unfounded, yet they go unchallenged. So when you hear yourself thinking such self-judgments, ask yourself, "How do I know this is true?"

> **DEEPER WISDOM**
>
> Your negative beliefs about yourself also harm you in the eyes of others. People will detect your self-beliefs, and they will sense your related feelings of inadequacy as well. Then they will value you accordingly. The simple logic is that people will value you similarly to how you value yourself. They will take their cues from you.

You may believe your tough self-criticism strengthens you and makes you work harder. But that's just your false shame trying to justify itself and control you. Your self-disapproval actually undermines your confidence, feeds your false shame, and therefore weakens you. So when you hear your self-deprecatory beliefs emerge, consider it your duty to challenge them. They are as much a threat to you as attacks made by others questioning your competence and denouncing you. Therefore, just as you would appropriately defend against unjust external critiques and state the truth, defend yourself against unfair internal critiques as well.

Many people I encounter, and especially leaders, also belittle themselves by dismissing and discounting their many achievements. They barely acknowledge them and instead focus on what they have not yet done. Do you do that, too? You may think this is helpful as it keeps you focused on your goals. But that is an irrational belief, too. It's your false shame trying to justify itself again. When you fail to honor what you've done so far, you deprive yourself of the self-esteem your prior achievements can provide you.

I came to know a senior executive who grew up in a poor, working-class family. He was the first to graduate from high school and then worked as a machinist in an oil refinery, a significant accomplishment in the eyes of his family. He went much further, though, attending college and ultimately achieving at very high professional levels. Yet, he would compare himself with his executive colleagues and in some small ways continuously find himself lacking. Others complained he lacked sufficient confidence and passion. But really, the problem was his distorted self-perception.

He told me he was beleaguered by recurring dreams of returning to his old job at the refinery. "It's always the same in the dream," he said. "I see all my old coworkers there and they say to me, 'We knew you would come back.' And I say, 'Yeah, I guess this is where I really belong.'"

Clearly, his self-doubt had a strong hold on him. To help him overcome it, I suggested he was in a long-jump competition. But unlike his peers, his starting point was many feet back. Although he'd had far fewer resources than they had enjoyed, he leaped so far forward that he had drawn even with them. His leap, therefore, was much greater than theirs. "You know," he said, "I'd never seen it that way." With this new perspective and by continuously questioning his old views of himself, my client came to see he'd been carrying around an inaccurate self-appraisal. He came to see his false shame more clearly and began to free himself from it.

When I last heard from him, he told me of yet another extraordinary step in his career he had just taken. This had doubled both his responsibilities and his income. He then added, "Remember those dreams I used to have about going back to the refinery? They're all gone now. You know, I think I've finally defeated that irrational self-doubt."

Many people, in at least some areas, have had starting points far behind those of their peers. Usually, these are the very areas in which they have challenged themselves greatly, yet now judge themselves harshly.

Does that describe you, too? Which of your uneven starting points are you not now acknowledging? Perhaps you are judging yourself by the distance from where you aspire to be rather than by how far you have already come. That is very unfair to you. And it undermines your confidence and therefore your power.

To correct your false beliefs about yourself, there are several specific approaches you can use. First, expose the beliefs by making them visible on paper or in another medium directly in front of you. So when the voice of the false shame tells you, for example, "You've hardly accomplished anything at all," write down that statement. Then take a moment to look at what you have written. When the false belief is no longer swirling inside your head but is placed at a distance outside of you, you have more power over it. From your new perspective, you can begin to see that it's actually a distortion.

When you have identified a shaming belief and have written it down, next collect all the evidence that relates to its accuracy. If, for example, you believe, "I'm not very good at what I do," consult the actual data and write it out in front of you. List all of your relevant successes and achievements. Include the other evidence that disproves the belief and the evidence that tends to support it too. Seeing all the facts on paper will clarify your thinking. Your belief that was hounding you may begin to appear ludicrous.

Also consider collecting relevant information from others that you trust. Just as you need others to tell you where you are blocking your power, you also need them to tell you your talents and gifts. This is because, in both cases, you likely cannot see yourself clearly.

I personally used this approach to help me write this book. My self-doubt was telling me I had little of importance to say. But when I asked my colleagues, they had a much different view. Consulting with them helped me gain a perspective different from my self-doubt. I came to see my self-doubt was not "me," but just a voice I did not have to believe.

What I say here about false beliefs does not mean you have no limitations. Like all people, you probably have your share. But notice how your false shame magnifies them. Your beliefs around them are likely holding you back more than the limitations themselves.

Look carefully, then, at the beliefs that fuel your false shame. When you hold your power in objectively appraising them, they will dissipate and even disappear. You need not believe everything you hear, especially when it's coming from inside of you. By protecting yourself against what's not true, you enable yourself to be more powerful.

summary

KEY POINTS TO REMEMBER

- Your false shame is based on beliefs about yourself that are likely untrue.

- You may think your self-critical beliefs help you and make you work harder. But really, your self-criticism undermines your confidence and weakens you. You are more powerful when your efforts are not driven by feelings of inadequacy and self-doubt.

- To correct the beliefs driving your false shame, listen for them when your self-doubt emerges. When you identify them, write them out in front of you. This gives you a distance from your beliefs that allows you to more clearly assess them.

- For each belief you identify, list the evidence that supports it, and the evidence that counters it as well. As you assess the evidence, the belief will likely appear to be quite distorted.

- In evaluating your beliefs about yourself, also consider asking for the views of others you trust. This can be helpful as it is very difficult to view yourself clearly.

- As you take these steps and challenge the beliefs supporting your false shame, both the beliefs and the false shame will dissipate and even disappear.

ACTIONS TO ENHANCE YOUR POWER

- At least three times over the course of the next week, notice when you are feeling inadequate or are otherwise feeling badly about yourself. If you notice those feelings right now, start doing this exercise now as well. Each time you notice these feelings, ask yourself, "What am I believing about myself that is triggering my self-doubt? What am I telling myself?" Write down the beliefs you identify. Then, next to each belief, write out all the relevant evidence that supports it, and that which discredits it, too. After you've written out the evidence and have reviewed it, ask yourself, regarding each belief, "What does the evidence show? What would a reasonable and compassionate person determine to be true?" Notice the effect your answers have on the feelings of inadequacy that, moments ago, were active within you.

- Identify three beliefs you have about yourself that cause you to feel inadequate. For example, your may believe, "I have not accomplished much" or "I am not very likable." Then identify three people you trust highly, whom you can be vulnerable with and whom you think would honestly and compassionately provide you information about yourself. Approach these individuals separately and tell them the beliefs you identified. Ask them to what extent they agree or disagree with the beliefs. This exercise puts you in a vulnerable position, but it can provide you information that powerfully negates and unravels some of your most negative beliefs about yourself. As a result, you may experience a significant lessening of your false shame.

COUNTER THE SELF-REJECTION OF
FALSE SHAME WITH DEEP SELF-ACCEPTANCE

Recognize the False Shame	Correct Distorted Beliefs	Deepen Your Self-Acceptance	Develop Your Humility	Take Action

You are rejecting yourself when you yield to your feelings of inadequacy. The antidote for these feelings, then, is deep self-acceptance. So instead of condemning yourself for your current limitations, accept them even while you work to change them. Your self-acceptance implies that you treat yourself with kindness and compassion—and that protects you from falling into more negative states that can harm you. As you more fully accept yourself, the manifestations of your false shame will subside in equal measure. You will become less fearful of rejection, less perfectionistic, and less interested in nonproductive competition. This will free up your energies and your passion.

Your false shame is actually a form of self-rejection. When you feel inadequate, when you immerse yourself in self-doubt, when you say, "I don't have what it takes," you are rejecting yourself as not worthy. And that rejection harms you. It undermines your self-esteem and confidence, and therefore your power. It also undermines your leadership. If you don't accept yourself, how can you expect others to accept you? A potent antidote for your self-rejection, then, is self-acceptance—a deliberate choice to accept yourself just as you are.

We talked about self-acceptance in Chapter 2, but because it's so crucial to resolving false shame, we need to address it here too. Remember that self-acceptance does not mean you are collapsing into your limitations and giving up on growing. Rather, it means that you are accepting your limitations even as you work to change them.

Remember, also, that self-acceptance implies you are being compassionate with yourself. When you get lost in your false shame, you are being unkind instead. In fact, your self-rejection is naturally painful to you. It takes you into negative emotional states and keeps you in them. Your compassionate self-acceptance, on the other hand, actually protects you. By enhancing your confidence and your mood, it lifts you out of your negative states that can damage your relationships and impair you.

As you come to accept yourself as you are, the different manifestations of false shame will release their grip on you. For example, if you fear rejection, you will find that your kind self-acceptance dramatically decreases that fear.

One amiable and animated marketing consultant felt hurt and rejected whenever potential clients refused his services. So to protect himself, he became rather stiff and formal in entering new relationships. "I felt my personal style was not acceptable to a lot of people in the corporate world," he explained to me, "so I decided to change it." He was responding to his false shame by becoming enclosed and self-protective.

Ultimately, as he found, this inauthentic approach was not effective. So after much intense frustration, he reversed course with his prospective clients, opened up, and became more self-revealing. Accordingly, he became more personable and easier to connect with. Many reacted quite favorably and this brought him significantly more business. He said to me, "I'm not for everyone. But in the end, I just had to be me." He could tolerate whatever outcomes arose because he was committed to liking and accepting himself regardless.

Other people who fear rejection may react to their false shame by trying too hard. They have something to prove, which is their own self-worth. Naturally, their prospective clients—or prospective mates—are not comfortable with their tense self-absorption. The feared rejection, then, is even more likely to happen.

So if you fear rejection as many people do, ask yourself, "How am I dealing with my fear? Do I protect myself and close myself off? Or do I try too hard?" Either way, you're not really connecting. And you're likely setting yourself up for more rejection. So consider instead simply accepting yourself just as you are. You will likely find that as you accept yourself more, others will, too. And from that stance of self-acceptance, you will build relationships that are more authentic and enduring.

If your feelings of inadequacy make you want to do things perfectly, your compassionate self-acceptance will help you here too. As you fully accept yourself as you are, you will no longer need to appear so exceptional when that doesn't benefit you. You will know where the boundary lies between "good enough" and inefficiency. Large swaths of time, previously devoted to unnecessary perfection, may start opening for you. Any excessive time you've been spending polishing your creations—or your appearance—can then be spent in other activities that better serve you.

If you deplete your energies with unproductive competition, your greater self-acceptance will help you here as well. You will have less to prove and therefore less of a need to compete when that doesn't benefit you.

- "Am I willing to view myself with compassion?"
- "Am I willing to accept rather than condemn whatever I see?"
- "Am I willing to forgive myself?"

Your compassionate self-acceptance will be especially helpful for your overall self-awareness. As we've discussed, observing your mistakes and how they limit you can be painful. It may activate your false shame in such strong degree that you avoid looking. But your kind self-acceptance protects you against your false shame so that you're more willing and able to see yourself clearly. Ask yourself, then, "Am I willing to look at myself with compassion—and accept rather than condemn whatever I see? Am I willing to forgive myself?" Your answers are crucial to your growth and to your greater power.

KEY POINTS TO REMEMBER

- When you fall into a state of false shame, you are actually rejecting yourself. The antidote, therefore, is complete self-acceptance.

- As we discussed in Chapter 2, self-acceptance means that you are not condemning yourself for your limitations, but are accepting them even as you work to change them.

- Self-acceptance also implies that you are being kind and compassionate with yourself. This protects you from negative states that can otherwise harm you.

- Your compassionate self-acceptance will diminish the manifestations of your false shame such as your fear of rejection, your perfectionism, and any unproductive competition. This will release your energies for other activities that better serve you.

ACTIONS TO ENHANCE YOUR POWER

- Set aside 20 minutes to reflect. Identify at least two or three aspects of yourself that are difficult for you to accept. Once you have identified these items, notice the negative feelings about them and about yourself that arise and begin to swirl around within you. Then take the following steps.

  - Ask yourself, "Is my refusal to accept these things about myself really serving me? Or might it be harming me?" Try adopting a kinder and more accepting view of yourself. You might say, for example, "I'm really doing the best that I can" or, "I'm not going to condemn myself for this anymore."

  - Make a commitment that at least for the next week, whenever you hear self-criticism about these items, you will repeat your statements of self-acceptance. Then see what effect that has on your confidence and your power.

  - Remind yourself that your self-acceptance does not mean you are giving up on changing these things. Instead, you are only being kinder and less condemning of yourself so that you can actually make the changes when you are ready to do so.

DEEPEN YOUR DIGNITY WITH HUMILITY AND THE CONNECTEDNESS THAT COMES WITH IT

Recognize the False Shame > Correct Distorted Beliefs > Deepen Your Self-Acceptance > **Develop Your Humility** > Take Action

You may respond to your false shame by seeking to be superior to other people. That strategy is unlikely to succeed and is not sustainable. So consider instead adopting an attitude of humility. That would flow from your understanding that you and all others are fundamentally equal. When you no longer need to be "better than" anyone, you will find you no longer have concerns about being "less than" anyone, either. Humility, then, is a powerful cure for your feelings of inadequacy. Together with deep self-acceptance, it propels the transformation of your self-doubt into dignity. Humility also affirms your shared bond with all people and connects you more with them. That greater connectedness, and your greater warmth toward others that naturally follows, will further transform your false shame and heighten your self-value.

Your false shame can have you thinking, "I am fundamentally less than other people." But that is a difficult thought to bear. So as a compensation, you may tell yourself, "Actually, I am better than other people." But that perception is difficult to sustain as well. So you may find yourself spinning back and forth between these two opposing views of yourself, driven by your false shame. This will only pain you and deplete your power.

Your most powerful response to this quandary is to affirm, "In reality, I am fundamentally equal to all." This is the voice of your humility. It tells you that, essentially, you are no better and no worse than others. As you accept being equal to everyone, you are liberated from your efforts to be better than anyone. In that state of humility, you no longer have anything to prove.

> **definition**
>
> **HUMILITY**
> Conducting yourself based on the understanding that you are fundamentally equal to all people.

Then you can stop comparing yourself with others and stop activating your false shame. And you can stop judging yourself by standards that oppress you. With humility, you can more fully accept yourself just as you are. That lessens your self-doubt and heightens your self-value.

When you act with complete self-acceptance and humility, the result will be a palpable sense of your own dignity. As shown on the Five Gifts Roadmap, this emerges from the transformation of your false shame. Self-acceptance neutralizes the self-rejection of false shame. And humility neutralizes the opposite—the unsustainable self-inflation also triggered by false shame. When you neither denigrate yourself nor seek to elevate yourself above others, your consequent dignity will provide you great self-respect, and therefore great power.

> **definition**
>
> **DIGNITY**
> The demonstration of profound self-respect. It results from the combination of complete self-acceptance and humility.

A highly successful entrepreneur shared with me her encounters with this challenge. She moved in elite circles that included people even more successful than she and this was triggering her feelings of inadequacy. So when she was with them, she labored to demonstrate her worth. "I would talk about who I know, I'd talk about my successes, I'd talk about what I'm going to do. I was trying so hard to impress them and be someone I wasn't. Then I'd come home feeling nauseated and icky.

"After a while," she said, "I realized they're really no different from me. They have to brush their teeth just like me. They get happy and sad just like me. And they're going to get old and die just like me. So why would I put them above me—or try to compete against them? Now, I'm simply myself around them."

This executive had initially responded to her self-doubt in a way that limited her relationships. That is a very common pattern. Are you doing something like that, too? For example, do you act on your false shame by needlessly comparing yourself with others and trying to match them? Are you excessively focused on performing better than those around you? Look carefully, as you may be hurting yourself and blocking your power. Consider instead showing greater humility. Then observe what benefits flow back to you.

You will find that your greater humility actually aids you considerably in joining with others. And that expanded connectedness will even further decrease your feelings of inadequacy. When you feel connected to people, you are less likely to feel inadequate in relation to them. So try extending yourself more toward others. Then watch and see what happens.

Even better, from the foundation of your humility, show greater warmth and compassion toward others as well. Likely, your sense of your worth and dignity will grow even greater. This is a law of human nature. As you increasingly treat others with care and respect, you will feel ever more respect and care for yourself. As you increasingly honor others' value, you will increasingly know your own.

The person who most demonstrated humility to me was a close friend and mentor of mine, 35 years my senior. He was a carpenter who, when still young, had been orphaned. Yet, by the time of his death, he had amassed a considerable fortune. But he did little to advertise his abilities or success. He drove around town in a very modest car barely big enough for his large frame, and judging from his appearance, I sometimes wondered if he had more than two or three shirts in his closet. He was so focused on what he could do for others that he paid little attention to what people thought of him. As a result, his dignity simply shined through. And an ease and grace was visible in nearly all of his efforts.

> **POWER TALK (to self)**
>
> - "I don't need to try so hard anymore to be better than anyone else."
> - "We're all fundamentally equal."
> - "How would I be acting right now if I remembered all of my inherent dignity?"

Imagine what you could accomplish with such an ease and grace and dignity. Imagine the trust you would inspire. It starts with compassionately accepting yourself as you are. It continues with your humility—seeing yourself as no better than and no less than other people. Recognizing your true place among others, you will no longer need to struggle against yourself or struggle against them. As you practice self-acceptance and humility, your false shame will be progressively transformed.

You may have thought that humility is an acknowledgment of your unworthiness. But really, it is a powerful affirmation of your shared bond with all people. And it is a potent remedy for your false shame. It is therefore a crucial source of your power.

KEY POINTS TO REMEMBER

- Humility is based on your understanding that you are not fundamentally better than anyone else—and not fundamentally less than anyone, either. When you accept being equal to everyone, you no longer have anything to prove. Humility, therefore, is a powerful cure for your false shame.

- Humility combined with deep self-acceptance yields dignity. As shown on the Five Gifts Roadmap, dignity is the product of the transformation of your false shame.

- Humility will also help you be more connected with others. When you are more connected to people and when you show them greater warmth and compassion, your feelings of self-worth will naturally increase even further.

ACTIONS TO ENHANCE YOUR POWER

- At least once every day for the next week, offer a smile, a hello, or other words of kindness to a person whose social status is so different from yours that you would normally not interact with him or her. This may be, for example, a clerk, someone cleaning the sidewalk, or a homeless person. You might remind yourself prior to each interaction, "This person and I are fundamentally equal." After you have these exchanges, ask yourself, "What am I feeling right now?" Notice the likely positive impact of the experience on your self-worth. Notice the positive effect on your overall mood as well.

TAKE ACTION TO CONCLUSIVELY DISPROVE
YOUR IRRATIONAL SELF-DOUBT

| Recognize the False Shame | Correct Distorted Beliefs | Deepen Your Self-Acceptance | Develop Your Humility | Take Action |

As the final step in the transformation of your false shame, take action despite what it tells you. This is one of the most powerful things you can do. Yet, as you move forward and push into your self-doubt, its voice at first will likely grow louder. Especially then, don't back off but keep moving forward. In doing so, you will prove that you, rather than your false shame, are stronger. Probably, your action will also prove that the messages of your self-doubt are grossly untrue. Your self-doubt may continue to arise even after you've repeatedly defeated it. But its voice will have diminishing power.

When your false shame arises, summon all your strength and take action despite what it tells you. Likely, your action will prove that the messages of self-doubt are not true. Every time you so act, you will enhance your power and your false shame will grow smaller. This principle of taking action is easy to explain but difficult to follow.

For example, do you know people who, nearly every time you see them, talk about what they *want* to do but never do it? Perhaps they want to start a new business. Or begin a new career. Or develop a creative talent. You may have offered them advice, encouragement, and more. But still, nothing happens. Perhaps you've concluded that these people are "lazy" or "just can't" do what is necessary. Perhaps they have come to believe the same things about themselves, too. But none of this is likely true. What really holds them back is that they heed their own false shame and thereby cripple their power.

Now, instead of looking outward, look inward. Are you one of those people, too? Likely, there are many instances in which you have conquered your self-doubt, but are there other areas in which it is conquering you? Do you tell others—or tell yourself—what you will *someday* do, and never do it? Are there things you secretly and deeply want to do, but you hold back on account of your self-doubt? Do not berate yourself for this. Do not add even more to your false shame. Instead, just notice your predicament. Simply seeing it and knowing you have a choice will empower you.

Perhaps you have already taken a step or two in the direction of your goal. If so, you may have encountered one of the principal qualities of false shame: As you begin to challenge it and take action despite what it tells you, it will likely grow dramatically larger—before it ultimately yields to you. So as you contemplate approaching your employer and asking for more responsibility, or approaching investors to fund your new venture, or approaching the woman or man you want to marry, or approaching any other goal that will expand your existence, the voice of self-doubt will probably get increasingly active and frantically try to stop you.

Your central challenge at such times is to keep on moving despite what your false shame is telling you. You will hear it say things like, "I can't do this, I'm going to fail." Simply notice these voices and acknowledge them. And then keep on moving forward even as they grow louder. You will finally reach a point where you prove that you, not your false shame, are in control. Then its voice will grow quieter.

At other times and in other instances, your false shame may get active again. But as you refuse to heed it time after time, it will just be a voice with very little power. A CEO who built a thriving business told me he still sometimes hears the voice of self-doubt pestering him. It whispers to him that all he built may "come tumbling down." Sometimes, it even awakens him at three or four in the morning. The voice gets especially active when he's about to break through to his next level of success. Instead of panicking and reacting, he simply acknowledges, "There it goes again." And then he keeps on moving forward. He knows his false shame only has the power he lets it have over him.

So when your false shame arises, first rationally assess its messages to confirm they're probably invalid. Then take the necessary action despite what those messages tell you. Throughout your encounters with false shame, remember that it is your steady presence and onward movement that continuously defeat it.

I personally have a tendency to let my self-doubt control me. If I am not vigilant, I will retreat in the face of it until I'm enclosed in a small and unhappy prison cell of my own false shame. However constricted I find myself, though, I know I can always push forward into the self-doubt and gain back my freedom. Many of my most important successes and relationships have come from my doing so. This book would not exist if I had not repeatedly pushed into and through my false shame.

Make this your mantra, then, your constant refrain: "I will take action despite my false shame." Usually, you will find this leads to far greater success than what your self-doubt was advising you. But even when your actions do not get you to your goal, this will still be a victory for you. That's because by taking action regardless of your self-doubt, you will have enhanced your free will and your power. You will have diminished the rule of false shame over you. Nearly always, this is more important to your long-term success and happiness than the outcome of a single effort.

So when you hear the voice of self-doubt emerging, ask yourself, "What next steps will make me most powerful?" Then take the necessary action. One of your most important investments in your own success is to continuously move forward despite your false shame.

---

summary

KEY POINTS TO REMEMBER

- The final step in the transformation of your false shame is taking action despite what it tells you. When you do so, your self-doubt will likely intensify. At such times, be sure to continue moving forward. Ultimately, the self-doubt will subside and yield to you.

- When you take action contrary to your self-doubt, you will prove that its messages to you are untrue. You will also prove that you, rather than your self-doubt, are in control.

- As you repeatedly take action despite your false shame, it may still emerge from time to time. But its authority over you will be decidedly weaker. Your dignity will be more apparent and you will have more power.

ACTIONS TO ENHANCE YOUR POWER

- Take some time alone with yourself where you will have no distractions. Sit comfortably, take several deep breaths, and let yourself relax. After a few moments of simply breathing, start reflecting on what you *want* to do but, because of your self-doubt, haven't been doing. Make a list of the items that come to mind that are important and meaningful for you. For each item, confirm that practical constraints such as time and money are not preventing you from taking action. Be careful, though, because your self-doubt may masquerade as concerns about practical issues. Once you have created your list, do the following:

  - Select one item you are willing to take action on. To ease into this and avoid overwhelming yourself, consider selecting an item that only moderately activates your self-doubt when you imagine doing it.

  - For the item you select, identify the beliefs underlying your self-doubt and confirm that they are likely invalid. For this purpose, you may want to use the tools provided in the second section of this chapter. If you cannot make this confirmation, select a more appropriate item from your list.

  - Next, identify the first step you are willing to take to fulfill your identified desire. Make the step as small as it needs to be for you to actually take it and begin moving forward. For example, your first step may be spending an hour doing some research or it may be preparing what you will say to a person whose support you need.

  - After you have completed your first step, then take another in the same way. And then another. And so on until you are actually doing the very thing that your self-doubt was keeping you from. As you encounter the likely intensification of false shame and other emotions, use the tools in this book for managing those emotions and moving through them.

  - Once you have completed one item on your list, then take on another. As you continue addressing these challenges, watch your self-doubt shrink and your power expand.

5

TRANSFORM YOUR
ANGER INTO COMPASSION

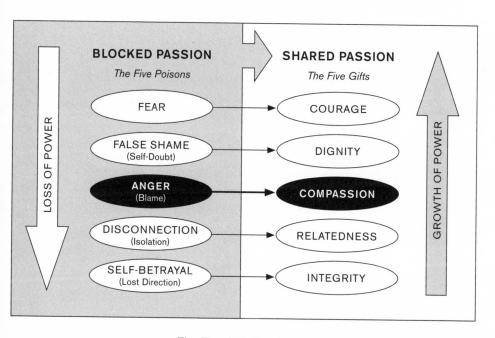

The Five Gifts Roadmap

ANGER IS DAMAGING YOUR RELATIONSHIPS AND BLOCKING YOUR POWER

Irritations and resentments are natural and predictable for anyone, including a leader. Yet, to the extent you indulge them, you are dissipating your power. Your expressions of anger and blame undermine your relationships with the very people you need in order to be most successful. Even indirect utterances of your resentments are noticed and erode others' trust in you. And any unexpressed resentments you harbor block the free flow of your passion. As a leader, you set the emotional tone in your organization. The people around you sense your emotional state and respond to it in kind. Consider, then, what you want your emotional impact to be.

If you are like most people and like most leaders, you sometimes express your anger. Perhaps you often do. You may believe this makes you more powerful, but that belief is dangerously untrue. Your anger actually impedes your effectiveness and harms you.

As you read this, are you seeing how this applies to you? Perhaps you are thinking, "But I'm not really an angry person. I just get a little frustrated or annoyed from time to time." But these emotions are still forms of anger. There are smaller degrees of anger and larger degrees. As you will see, a little anger blocks your power a little and a lot of anger blocks your power a lot. It is best if your power is not blocked at all.

It is natural and predictable, though, that you will get angry. As a human being, and all the more so if you are a leader, you are continuously working to make things happen. And you are continuously bumping up against obstacles along the way. You will naturally feel frustration as a result. The question is, what will you do with your frustration or your irritation once it arises? Will you let it determine your next words, your next actions? Or will you transform it, using the tools I will provide you, and be more powerful?

Before I give you those tools, let's first discuss how anger obstructs your power. Once you know these mechanisms, you can better guard against this danger inside of you. One way in which your resentments likely harm you is that they alienate you from the very people you need. Has your anger, in fact, disrupted and even destroyed relationships crucial for you? In your professional life? In your family or in your community? The harm that results is often tragic—and it typically occurs outside of awareness.

For instance, a CEO irately complained to me, "My people are not communicating with me; they're evading me." "Why do you think that's so?" I asked. She attributed their actions to their personal weakness and lack of maturity. But her team members told me a different story. They said she would angrily attack them when they stated opinions contrary to hers. Naturally, they were now angry themselves. They were expressing their resentment by avoiding her.

When I brought this information back to the CEO, she seemed annoyed and dismissed it as "whining." I asked, "Are you now angry at me?" She was taken aback and fell momentarily silent. Then, more quietly, she acknowledged, "I guess that's how I react when I get information I don't like." She was beginning to see how she was creating destructive cycles of anger between herself and the people around her. Using her words so pointedly, she was damaging her relationships with the very individuals she needed.

This particular leader was expressing her anger directly. Others do the same thing indirectly. How about you? How do you express your resentments? For example, do you complain to others about colleagues, family members, and friends who irritate you? Although you are not attacking them directly, you are still undermining your power. When people hear you express your resentments, they will take note and trust you less. They will wonder if you say similar things about them. And what they'll really be hearing is the leakage of your power. What they'll be hearing is, "Anger is controlling him rather than he controlling his anger."

If you let your anger spill out as blame, you will deplete your power even more. When you blame, when you say, "It's your fault," you are giving away responsibility. But responsibility—literally, the ability to respond—is actually your power. And when you blame others, you give that power away to the very people you are angry at. And by blaming them, you are angering them as well.

Unless I'm very careful, I'll indulge in blaming others, too. In one instance, an engagement with a new corporate client did not go as well as I had hoped. With a bit of irritation, I told myself that the people on the client's side were not prepared to do what was necessary. Although it felt satisfying to blame someone else, I wasn't quite believing my own story. Later, I was willing to look more closely at the role I played—and to tolerate the pain of doing so. I then clearly saw my own significant errors that had largely created the disappointing result. And I saw how I might create a better outcome the next time.

Look closely to see if you like to blame as well. It's a very common human habit. But be thoughtful before indulging it. Ask yourself, "How does blaming undermine my ability to make things better? How does it undermine my power?"

Perhaps you don't typically express your resentments overtly, but do so in a subtler manner. For example, when you are annoyed with a colleague, do you delay responding to her messages, or disregard them entirely? Or when you are disappointed in a friend's—or your spouse's—lack of support, are you a bit distant the next time you see him? Be honest with yourself. Aren't you trying to communicate your unhappiness by such actions? People are feeling the resentment, the emotional tone, that you are communicating. What impact will that have on your relationship? How will that block your power and harm you?

For example, the colleague waiting for a response to her message is feeling your irritation. Maybe she's not quite aware of it, but your resentment has registered. And because your emotions are contagious, now she's a little angry, too. If she's not very aware, she may put that anger into action. And that is a danger to you.

Sometimes, you may feel anger but not put it into words or actions. This is better, as it preserves more of your power. But still, even just feeling anger and languishing in those feelings is power-depleting for you. That's because the people around you will sense what you're feeling. You are not as good at hiding your emotions as you think. You give off the signals and people read them. You need to magnetize others with your leadership. Your anger has the opposite effect.

I worked with an executive who was exceptionally polished, but it was not very difficult to detect a certain edginess just beneath his surface. In fact, as I observed him speaking with his colleague about a difference of opinion, I had a strong visceral sense that a part of him wanted to leap out of his chair and strangle this man opposite him.

After the interaction, I asked the executive about his emotional state while in it. He replied, "I was actually feeling quite annoyed." "To the point," I asked, "that you even kind of felt like strangling your colleague?" His eyes opened wide. "How did you know that?" he asked. "I got this sense that you wanted to jump out of your chair and strangle him." "That's amazing," he said. "That is exactly what I was feeling." "It was kind of hard to miss," I responded.

Even if others don't detect your unexpressed resentment, it still blocks your passion. It sucks away your energy and distracts you. The brilliant flame you need to be is darkened for those moments you allow the anger to take you over. As the leader of your organization, you set the emotional climate. What do you want it to be? What climate is going to create the most passion and engagement?

Your challenge is not to be free of all anger. Your challenge is to be aware when it arises within you. And then to limit that anger and transform it as quickly as possible. So take some time today and reflect: "Where in my career, and in my life overall, has my anger destroyed things important to me?" This can be a difficult exercise, but it is crucial for you. To stop the destructive force of anger in your life, you must be aware of it. Once you see how your anger harms you and steals from you what is most important, then you can begin to master it.

KEY POINTS TO REMEMBER

- Anger, resentment, and blame are common and natural in people, especially in leaders. Likely, then, they are common in you too.

- Your expressions of anger deplete your power:

  - Anger harms your relationships with the people you need.

  - Anger expressed as blame also amounts to giving away responsibility, and therefore your power, to those you see at fault.

  - Your leadership needs to magnetize others, yet your anger has the opposite effect.

- Even unexpressed anger distracts you, dims your brilliance, and blocks your passion.

ACTIONS TO ENHANCE YOUR POWER

- At the end of every day for the next week, reflect on the following two questions: (1) "When did I get annoyed or irritated today?" (2) "What impact did that have on my colleagues and on how they might respond to me?" Then review your schedule for the next day and identify when your anger may get triggered again. For each of these potential trigger points, set an intention for how you will act. If you find this practice helpful, continue it at a level of frequency that works for you.

COMMENCE TRANSFORMING
YOUR ANGER BY SELF-POSSESSION

| Be Self-Possessed | Strive for Understanding | Demonstrate Compassion | Practice Forgiveness |

The first step in transforming your anger is self-possession. This means, literally, that you possess yourself rather than letting your irritations and resentments possess you and govern your words and your actions. Being self-possessed means that you are calm, focused, and in control. You will grow increasingly self-possessed as you practice noticing your anger as it emerges and then deliberately choosing not to act on it despite the temptation. You will be even more self-possessed if you are aware of the triggers for your anger. Then you can anticipate it and guard against it from even arising. Many of your triggers will likely involve feeling offended and disrespected and, more deeply, your unwarranted feelings of inadequacy.

Now that you know how anger saps your power, let's talk about how to transform it. On the Five Gifts Roadmap, this is the path of transforming anger into compassion. Actually, four steps are involved, as shown above. The first step, and a crucial one, is self-possession.

Being self-possessed means, literally, that you possess yourself rather than your emotions possessing you. You, not your emotions, are in control. If you are self-possessed, you may still feel angry. But you will notice that anger and, importantly, not act on it. The opposite is your automatically and without thought, even reflexively, putting your anger into words and actions. So someone pokes you and, reflexively, you react in anger. The problem for leaders is that people are always poking them. The challenge is to stay self-possessed despite these provocations.

For example, a board member says at a meeting, "You have made terrible mistakes in implementing your strategy." If you just notice the anger that may well up inside of you

but don't act on it, then you are controlling the anger rather than it controlling you. Then, in that self-possessed state, you can very calmly and without the slightest irritation say to the accusatory board member, "Tell me what you see as the significant mistakes and let us talk about it." In this way, you hold your power. The board member will know she's provoked you greatly and yet you are unperturbed. She will think to herself, "This man is powerful. I throw rocks at him and he is unruffled. I can trust him to run this company."

To be self-possessed and powerful in this way, you must be self-aware. I introduced the topic of self-awareness in Chapter 1 and it's important that we return to it here. At a minimum, self-awareness in this context means you are aware when you are angry. You may say, "Of course I know when I'm angry." My work with leaders tells me this may not always be so.

If you carefully observe yourself, you may notice frustrations, irritations, and resentments spilling out into your words and actions. And much of this usually happens outside your awareness. Sometimes, this will all be obvious to you once you stop and look. Often, it will be more subtle. None of this is surprising if you are working in a high-pressure and competitive environment. Still, though, it undermines your capacity to be self-possessed. Your lack of awareness depletes your power.

For instance, you may hardly be aware that you resent a colleague and then offend her by not thinking to invite her to a meeting. Or you may not be conscious of holding a past resentment toward a person, yet the way you greet him is slightly stiff, a bit removed, almost imperceptibly so. Even though you might not be aware of your resentments in these situations, you are telegraphing them. And on some level, they register with their target. The individual will feel slighted by your conduct and you will have further driven a wedge in your relationship.

When you act in these ways, you seed your relationships with little droplets of poison. And you are only dimly aware, or not aware at all, of what you are doing. So ask yourself, "Toward whom do I feel resentment? How might I be letting that leak out?"

> **POWER TALK (to self)**
>
> • "Whom do I feel resentful toward?"
>
> • "How is that resentment coming out?"
>
> • "How can I respond to my resentment in a way that is most powerful?"

Sometimes, you will not be aware of your anger until you have already acted on it. Even at that point, your awareness will be helpful. You are more powerful, though, when you are aware of your anger before you put it into words and actions. Then you can stop the anger from taking you over and controlling your conduct. Holding your power in this way, you stand at a distance from the anger, observing it, knowing it's not you. Then you can deliberately decide, "What do I want to do with this emotion? How can I respond in a way that most preserves my power?" This is true self-possession.

You will be even more self-possessed and powerful when you are aware of the triggers for your anger. Then you will be better equipped to anticipate it and guard against it. Those triggers may be team members failing to deliver on their commitments to you. Or the triggers may be your children not doing what you have requested of them repeatedly. Or the trigger may be some other obstruction to the accomplishment of your objective. Knowing these triggers can be helpful, but they are not always under your control.

More helpful is knowing the deeper triggers for your anger. These triggers are inside of you, and therefore they are entirely under your control. These deeper triggers are your feelings of being offended and disrespected. Nearly all your anger has roots at this level within you. The obstacles people throw in your path would not be nearly as provocative for you if you did not react on this emotional level.

For example, a peer withholds her cooperation from you. This stymies your progress and you get resentful. Is all your anger simply due to the objective fact of this obstacle? Or does your anger also result, even largely so, from your emotional reaction to the hindrance—from your feeling dishonored and disrespected?

An especially driven executive would get very annoyed when the members of his staff failed to meet their commitments. However, in our work together, we saw that the particular deadlines his people missed were nearly always inconsequential impediments to the continued growth of the business. We saw that if similar impediments resulted from natural forces, like the weather, he would not be angry at all. His anger, we discovered, was actually the result of his feeling offended that his people had failed to keep their promises to him.

"Doesn't that give away your power?" I asked. "What do you mean?" he replied. "I mean you're letting other people's conduct drag you into emotional states where you feel tense and irate." "But," he said, "they're breaking their promises to me. That's disrespectful." "That's about them," I said, "and you don't have to take it personally. As the CEO, you have to enforce their commitments. But you don't have to get angry. In fact, maybe you also have to keep your cool so that you can be most effective." He reflected for a moment and replied, "Let me think that over."

Over the ensuing months, he worked hard to gradually shift his habitual mode of reacting. As he later said to me, "Why should I let other people's actions govern how I feel? No wonder I was angry 80 percent of the time." He smiled and added, "I think I've now gotten it down to about 40 percent." Although it was a joke, we both knew it was not too far from the truth. Changing our habits takes time.

My experience with executives shows this CEO's prior reactions are a common pattern. When they feel disrespected, they very often get angry. Is that your pattern, too? If so, notice how you are giving away your power. Notice how you are letting others' conduct "make" you feel disrespected and angry. Observe, in those moments, that you are not self-possessed. Rather, others' actions and your emotional reactions to them are "possessing" you. As you become more aware of this, you can take back your power.

If the pattern I am describing fits you, its underlying cause is your unwarranted feelings of inadequacy. It is your false shame. If you were to truly recognize your own value, it would be impervious to others' words and actions. You would not be triggered by their disrespectful conduct.

So you have a path toward reclaiming your full power. Using the approaches in the previous chapter, you can transform your false shame and know your true value independent of others' behaviors. But until you do so, you will be susceptible to feelings of inadequacy. And then you may respond to those feelings with anger. The anger will be easier for you to feel and easier to express than the feelings of false shame. That's because the anger makes you feel more powerful—even though that power is an illusion.

Many people do not see this deeper cause of their anger. Instead, they insist, "No, when someone disrespects me, I will naturally get angry." Is that your view, too? If so, notice how that disempowers you. You are giving to others the power to determine your value, your emotional state, and your dignity. And you are not giving it away to just anyone. Sometimes, in fact, you are giving that power to the very people who wish to belittle you and undermine you. In effect you are saying, "Let

me find my enemies and allow my worth to be determined by their actions." But this is exactly what so many people do. And it greatly harms them.

To break free of this pattern is very difficult. You will probably not do it all at once. And like most people, you may never be entirely free of it. But at least you can create greater degrees of freedom for yourself. You can gradually lessen your vulnerability to provocations and to being pushed off balance. And you can grow toward a vision of yourself as being calm and dignified regardless of others' conduct.

KEY POINTS TO REMEMBER

- Being self-possessed requires both self-awareness and a deliberate choice to not let your anger control you.

- At a minimum, the requisite self-awareness includes your being aware of your resentments before acting on them.

- Ideally, your self-awareness will also include your being aware of the deeper causes of your anger—your feeling disrespected and your related, unwarranted feelings of inadequacy.

- Being self-aware in these ways allows you to make more conscious choices and therefore to be more self-possessed. This renders you more powerful.

ACTIONS TO ENHANCE YOUR POWER

- In the next week, exercise your self-possession muscle by noticing, in the moment, when you are feeling annoyed or angry. Try not to act on the anger, but just notice it instead. See how well you can maintain your composure and self-control. Do this at least three times. Then notice the inner strength you feel as a result.

- Recall two or three times recently when you felt angry in your work. For each incident, reflect on what "made" you angry. Did you feel offended and disrespected by a colleague's conduct? Consider the notion that the conduct was really about him or her, not you. See if that helps you feel any differently about the incident.

FURTHER TRANSFORM YOUR ANGER BY UNDERSTANDING THOSE WHO PROVOKE YOU

| Be Self-Possessed | Strive for Understanding | Demonstrate Compassion | Practice Forgiveness |

The next step in transforming your anger is to understand the people at whom it is directed. Your current assumptions about them are likely incomplete and just not true. When you look more deeply, you will probably find that their behavior is driven by negative emotions and even by their own feelings of being disrespected and unworthy. You may also find that your actions have triggered those very feelings. This degree of insight will greatly aid you in protecting your relationships from the destructive impact of your anger.

When you are angry at someone, it's because you don't truly understand him. If you knew the full truth about him, you would not be angry. This relates to what I said earlier. It is your distorted perceptions that create your negative emotions. In this case, the distorted perceptions are incorrect assumptions you make about the meaning of people's actions.

For example, one executive was incensed that her colleague was not responding to her messages. I cautioned her, "Do you really know the reasons for this?" "I don't need to know the reasons," she shot back. "This is about a crucial issue we've been working on and I've left her three messages in 36 hours." She later did discover the reason, though. Her colleague's daughter had just attempted suicide and was in the hospital, seriously injured. My client was mortified and contrite.

So when you notice yourself getting angry at a colleague or a friend or your life partner, get curious instead. Ask yourself, "Why might this person be acting this way?" Take time to pause and reflect. Say to yourself, "I wonder what would cause this person to do this now?" Reflecting like this, rather than falling into anger, makes you more powerful.

In the prior section, I explained that feeling disrespected and feeling inadequate are the primary triggers for anger. So when someone is provocative and angry toward you, suspect these triggers are operating within him. Then, rather than getting angry yourself, you can respond more skillfully and effectively.

A CEO complained to me that an important lunch meeting with a potential partner had gone poorly. He recalled that it had even started with a negative feeling. He had reached out to shake hands and noticed that his counterpart's handshake was hard and icy. And he noticed a hard look in his eyes as well. "It sounds like he was angry," I said. "He was angry," my client replied, "but I can't understand why." The answer emerged, though, as we explored further.

My client remembered he had been annoyed that his counterpart had arrived at the restaurant ten minutes late. He expressed his irritation by remaining on his mobile phone call as this gentleman approached. He kept him waiting for only a brief moment or two. But it was enough to telegraph his resentment and plant seeds of poison. He acknowledged to me, "He kept me waiting, so I suppose I wanted to keep him waiting, too."

Let's look more closely at the chain of events, the final link in which was an aborted relationship. The initial triggering event was the lunch guest's being ten minutes late. My client reacted to this by feeling offended and disrespected and then getting angry. He failed to recognize that he really did not know why his lunch companion was late. It could have been for any of a number of different reasons. Perhaps he had a flat tire. Perhaps his wife had suddenly become sick and he needed to take her to the doctor. Perhaps he woke up terribly depressed that morning about his career and his life and was having great difficulty getting through his day.

This CEO did not consider any of these things. Instead—and largely because of his irrational feelings of inadequacy—he took the tardiness as a sign of disrespect and then acted out his resentment. The essence of his action was, "You made me feel disrespected; now I'm going to make you feel disrespected, too."

The prospective partner predictably reacted to the CEO's poison. He, too, felt disrespected and got angry. He showed it in his handshake and in his gaze. The CEO could have used these cues as signals about what was happening and what to do next. For example, noticing his colleague's anger, he might have identified its cause and addressed it by apologizing for the extended phone call. But he did not do this. Not surprisingly, the partnership they were meeting to discuss never happened.

This was all very painful for my client to see. It is so much easier to blame than to take responsibility. He saw that his uncontrolled resentment had effectively destroyed a nascent business relationship. He wondered with me: What else had he destroyed with his resentments? To safeguard and enhance your relationships—and your success—ask similar questions of yourself. Ask, "When have I triggered such emotional chain reactions?"

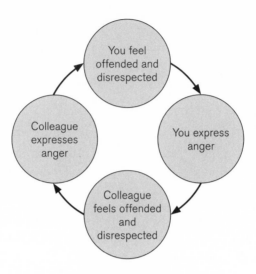

FIGURE 5.1 The Vicious Cycle of Feeling
Disrespected and Feeling Angry

As this story illustrates, when you express your anger toward people, they will likely feel offended. And then your anger will boomerang right back toward you. If you are not aware of what is happening, you will probably feel disrespected and offended and then express even more anger. You will be caught in a destructive, vicious cycle as shown in Figure 5.1.

This dynamic is a very common reason for destroyed relationships within organizations—as well as between spouses and friends. And the destruction of your relationships ultimately debilitates you and your power.

So when you feel disrespected, when you feel your anger beginning to well up, get curious instead. Search for understanding. Say to yourself, "I wonder what I might have done to trigger this person's conduct." Ask, "What have I created?" Remember that people will often treat you with anger or disrespect because they feel treated that way by you. Their

> **POWER TALK (to self)**
>
> - "I wonder what I may have done to trigger this person."
> - "It's not about me—it's not about my worth. But it may be about my actions."
> - "Look at what I created!"

perception may be distorted and inaccurate—or it may not be. You may find that you created the very situation you are now facing. This may be difficult for you to acknowledge. In fact, the more common pattern is to blame rather than to take responsibility.

For example, the CEO who talked on his phone as his counterpart stood waiting did not want to acknowledge that by acting on his anger, he had destroyed a potentially lucrative partnership. Feeling ashamed of his actions, he preferred to blame the other person instead. To stop blaming and take back his power, he had to quiet the shrill little accusatory voice of false shame deep inside. Then he could say, with dignity, "Yes, I created this outcome and I have learned from it. Next time, I can create a different result." When you, too, say calmly and without shame, "Look at what I created," you will have more power.

In the previous section, I said that when people treat you poorly, it's not really about you. Now I'm saying it really may be about you. Let me explain. People's conduct toward you is not about your worth. It's not about who you fundamentally are. In this sense, it's not about you. The point is to not take their conduct personally. But their reactions may well be about you in the sense of being emotionally fueled responses to your actions. So be aware of how you inadvertently or even deliberately trigger other people. With this understanding, you will be more effective with them and therefore more powerful.

So remember this important guideline: Instead of getting angry, get curious. Such curiosity can prevent much conflict. Conflict within organizations. Conflict between businesses. And conflict between nations. Instead of being provoked by others' angry and disrespectful acts, the leaders in these situations can choose to be curious instead. And so can you. "I wonder," you can say, "what is triggering this conduct on the other side. I wonder what I may have done to create these reactions." Being curious in this way will make you more powerful. And it will make your organization a better place in which to work. It will make the world a better place in which to live.

KEY POINTS TO REMEMBER

- Once you truly understand the causes of people's actions, it will be impossible for you to be angry with them. So don't believe your assumptions about the meaning of your colleagues' conduct. Instead, get curious why they're acting that way.

- When people are disrespectful or angry toward you, suspect that the cause may be your own inadvertent or intentional disrespect and anger directed toward them.

- Your blame of others may keep you from seeing how you created an unpleasant situation. Instead of blaming others or yourself, consider calmly getting curious about the part you played. That will enable you to create a different result next time.

ACTIONS TO ENHANCE YOUR POWER

- Recall at least two colleagues who have recently irritated you. In each case, write down your assumptions and beliefs about the causes of their conduct. Next, write down other potential causes for their behavior that cast them in a more neutral or positive light. The hypothesized causes may be a combination of emotional and objective factors. Then review the two lists of causes you created. Identify which causes, if you were to accept them as "working hypotheses," would most likely enhance your relationship. Consider adopting these hypotheses in order to increase your effectiveness.

- After you've done this exercise for past incidents, try doing it in the moment, informally, when you feel irritated at coworkers. Formulate hypotheses for their conduct that help you avoid being angry and therefore less effective.

DEEPEN THE TRANSFORMATION OF YOUR ANGER WITH COMPASSION

| Be Self-Possessed | Strive for Understanding | Demonstrate Compassion | Practice Forgiveness |

As you better understand those who trigger your anger, you will see their struggles and distress. If you respond with compassion, that will further transform your resentment. You will still be able to act as necessary in your leadership role, but your actions will no longer be fueled by anger. Compassion is a profoundly powerful stance because it allows you to be connected with people even when you must take action that negatively affects them. By showing such a human side of yourself, you enhance people's trust in you. One way to develop your compassion is through empathy—by sensing and imagining what others are feeling.

With understanding, you will see the distress inside of people that causes them to act in ways that provoke you. That distress will be some combination of their feelings of powerlessness, fear, anger, and inadequacy. The more hurtful and provocative people are, the more they are hurting inside. Seeing this clearly, you can choose to respond with compassion.

Responding this way means you are choosing kindness and concern. It means you are letting yourself be touched by another person's struggles. Compassion ensures that the transformation of your anger is more complete and enduring. When you are feeling compassion, it will be impossible for you to also be angry.

I'm not suggesting you use compassion because it's a nice thing to do. I'm suggesting you use it because it's one of the most powerful things you can do as a leader. Your success is dependent on the quality of your relationships. Compassion enhances them—and protects them from the frustrations, annoyances, and resentments so common between people. Anger depletes your energy and distracts you. Compassion, as the antidote to anger, keeps you more open and more energized, and therefore more powerful.

So when someone offends you, consider choosing compassion over anger. Consider asking yourself, "I wonder what pain inside is causing this person to act in this manner?" Being compassionate may sometimes feel difficult for you. But it renders you more trustworthy, more connected, and more effective.

Some leaders worry that being compassionate may make them weaker. But compassion does not stop you from taking the action your leadership requires. You can feel concern and kindness toward a person and still make decisions that negatively impacts him. As a leader, your concern for one person must be trumped by your concern for the greater whole that you serve. So you can have compassion for every member of your staff—and then dismiss them all if that's the necessary action.

At first, being compassionate might not seem like a very obvious response to a person's provocative behavior. For example, a vice president who was a fast-rising star in a large organization complained to me—with a great deal of agitation—that one of his colleagues reflexively and openly opposed him on nearly every issue. But I asked him one of my favorite questions: "What do you think could be the cause of his actions?"

"I don't know," my client said. "It's like he's always trying to compete with me. Maybe he feels insecure." He revealed that they had both started their careers from the same point many years back. But this vice president had progressed much further than his colleague—and the disparity was increasing. "Might he feel inadequate in comparison to you?" I asked. "I guess so," he replied. "Even humiliated?" "Well, that's kind of a strong word, but maybe," he responded. "I think," I concluded, "that your colleague's repeated challenges of you are only desperate and futile attempts to salvage his own self-esteem."

"Isn't that *his* problem?" my client asked. "It's your problem, too," I offered, "because he's undermining your leadership." I suggested to my client that a compassionate approach could make him more effective. As he considered this possibility, and considered his coworker's struggles too, he began to soften. His colleague's behavior was very extreme, but as he came to see, this only reflected how extreme was his suffering.

The next challenge, though, was to put this emerging compassion into action. We agreed on a plan for doing so. My client experimented with treating his colleague with more kindness, often endorsing his comments and seeking his input at meetings. Overall, he helped him look good and feel good in front of others. He was helping him restore some of his self-worth. The colleague's attacks mostly subsided, and this vice president was now a more gracious, confident, and powerful leader. "You know," my client said several months later, "he still sometimes annoys me, but not nearly as much as before. And now I have kind of a soft spot in my heart for him, too. He's really just doing the best that he can."

> **DEEPER WISDOM**
>
> When you act compassionately, you will also feel better about yourself. You will feel more in control, more generous, and less constricted. Your energy will flow more freely. As a result, you will be more powerful.

To increase your compassion, there are several things you can do. When you encounter someone who annoys you, consider telling yourself, "This could be me. If I were less self-aware, I could be the one acting in this way." You might even admit to yourself that you have indeed

- "What pain inside is caus-ing her to act this way?"
- "Given who she is, she's really doing the best that she can."
- "I've acted in similar ways myself."

acted in similar ways, at least at some point in your life. You might also tell yourself, "This person really is like me. He wants to be happy and successful, like me. And like me, he wants to avoid pain and distress and failure." And finally, consider saying to yourself, "This person is probably doing the best that he can."

An additional and very powerful tool for developing compassion is *empathy*. This is a deep form of understanding where you experience the other person's emotional state. You imagine what she is feeling and actually feel the same thing.

In order to develop empathy, first notice any negative thoughts and feelings you have about the other person and make a choice to set them aside, at least for a moment. Then imagine *being* this other person. Say to yourself, "I wonder what it feels like to be her." Or ask, "What is she feeling now that would cause her to act in these ways?" Or imagine *doing* the very things she is doing that you find so irritating—and then imagine what that would feel like.

With this kind of insight, you can actually see inside the people you need to relate to. And that makes you far more effective in your inter-actions with them. It makes you a far more powerful leader.

There's a potent shortcut to empathy. It builds on the principles dis-cussed in Chapter 2, that emotions are contagious and that people will often try to make you feel what they are feeling. So when you are in the

presence of a person you want to empathize with, simply get in touch with what you are feeling. If you notice an unpleasant emotion not typical for you, ask yourself, "Could this be what he is feeling?"

For example, you may notice that whenever you are around a certain friend or colleague, you feel irritable. Ask yourself, "Am I feeling *her* irritability? Is she trying to make me feel what she's feeling?" Your feelings will not be conclusive, but they'll give you very useful clues. Skilled psychologists frequently use this approach in their work.

Your empathy will do more than dispel your resentments. As you become more empathetic, people will notice and will trust you more. They will be more inclined to accept your leadership and will have greater loyalty toward you. Your effectiveness as a leader will therefore increase, too.

But don't just have compassion for others. Have compassion for yourself as well. Given the difficulties of daily life and the challenges of leadership, you need it and you deserve it. And this will protect you from any harsh self-criticism and therefore enhance your self-confidence as well as your power.

summary

KEY POINTS TO REMEMBER

- When you see the struggles and distress behind people's provocative actions, you can choose to respond with compassion. So responding means you are choosing kindness and concern. Compassion protects you from anger and the destructive harm it does to your relationships, your passion, and your power.

- Compassion does not stop you from taking necessary action. It only stops you from taking that action with anger.

- One way of developing compassion is through empathy. Empathy allows you to know and actually feel what others are feeling. This not only deepens the transformation of your anger, but also renders you more trustworthy and effective in your interactions overall.

- Consider being compassionate not just toward others, but with yourself as well. This will protect your self-esteem from debilitating self-criticism and therefore protect your power.

ACTIONS TO ENHANCE YOUR POWER

- Identify three people whom you sometimes judge negatively. Try to imagine what it's like to be them and the difficult emotions they may be enduring. Suggest to yourself, "Perhaps they're doing the best that they can." See if this replaces some of your judgment with compassion. Notice the impact that has on you and your leadership.

COMPLETE THE TRANSFORMATION
OF YOUR ANGER WITH FORGIVENESS

| Be Self-Possessed | Strive for Understanding | Demonstrate Compassion | Practice Forgiveness |

The final step in transforming your anger is forgiveness. To forgive means to let go of your resentments so that you can be more connected, more energized, and therefore more powerful. The difficulty of forgiveness is proportionate to its benefits. When you forgive, you prove to those observing you that you are larger than the circumstances that sometimes befall you. This will magnetize others to the power and presence of your leadership.

Forgiveness is the final step in transforming your anger. It means choosing to let go of your resentments in order to be more powerful. When you forgive, you let go of feeling offended and let go of your desire for retribution. You repudiate the division in your relationship. To forgive is a very wise business decision because otherwise, you are staying in your anger. And that anger blocks your passion and undermines your effectiveness.

> **definition**
>
> **FORGIVENESS**
> Choosing to let go of your anger and resentment—and thereby being more powerful.

Sometimes, it can be very difficult to forgive. People may have treated you in very thoughtless and demeaning ways. They may have caused you great harm. But if you truly understand these people and see their own distress that led them to cause such distress in you, then you can have compassion for them. And once you have such compassion, you can act on it by forgiving them.

Your forgiveness will be an act of generosity toward the person who offended you. But the greatest giving will actually be to yourself—because once you have released your anger, you will feel freer and have more energy and passion.

A CEO had trusted a senior member of her team with very sensitive information. Not long after, he departed. Using the information she had entrusted to him, he took her most prized customer with him. My client felt betrayed and was furious. For many months, she was preoccupied with her anger, and when she occasionally saw her former employee at industry events, she would get even more irate. She later confided in me, "I know this sounds a little extreme, but at times I'd imagine killing him."

Things came to a head when my client developed lower back pain, which grew progressively worse. "I used to say, 'My back is killing me,'" she said, "but, really, I knew it was my anger that was creating the pain. I realized then that either I was going to be bigger than this hatred, or it was going to control me and even destroy me. And that's when I chose to let it go and forgive him." Since that time, they have actually referred several new customers to each other.

A turning point in my own life centered on an act of forgiveness, too. A close acquaintance had terribly betrayed me and caused me great harm from which it took a long time to recover. The harm was not just financial. It was very much emotional as well. What

> **DEEPER WISDOM**
>
> Your refusal to forgive others will be hurtful to them, even to those who seem too callous to care. On some level, they will feel the sting of your rejection. Likewise, your forgiveness will relieve them. It will bring them back into the fold of your influence and leadership, rendering you all the more powerful.

made it worse was that she barely acknowledged she had done anything wrong at all. And yet I could not cut this person out of my life. We had a web of ties in the community that realistically could not be severed. I was stuck, laden down with feelings of resentment that were blocking my forward progress.

It was years before I was finally ready to forgive her. But even then, I knew I could not tell her my forgiveness. It would feel like an accusation for her and generate yet more anger. So I did what would have been unthinkable for me earlier. I actually asked for *her* forgiveness.

A powerful intuition told me this was the wisest and most powerful thing I could do. And I knew it was true—for several reasons. First, I realized I had indeed harmed this person. For the past years, in subtle and indirect ways, I'd been expressing my resentment toward her. I'd been feeding her my poison. So there really was something to seek forgiveness for. Second, by seeking her forgiveness, I was conclusively renouncing all my past resentments toward her. It was a powerful way of saying, "No more will I linger in this state of pain and depletion." Finally, I had come to see that she was angry at me for my resentment toward her. And I did not want her to continue being angry. I saw that it was harming her and harming our relationship. So I sought her forgiveness. And that level of forgiveness had a transformative impact on me.

> **POWER TALK (to self)**
>
> • "Whom can I forgive in order to free up my blocked energies?"

To forgive is one of the most powerful things you can do. It is a bold statement about your connectedness with others. And it is that connectedness that determines your success. You really are nothing without other people. If you wall out one person from your life, you are walling out a little part of everyone else. And that harms you and harms your leadership.

Forgiveness can be very difficult to achieve. It certainly was for me. And its difficulty is proportionate to its benefits. It tears down the walls between you and others. It frees you from the poisons of anger and resentment. It releases your energies so that you can accomplish all that you are destined to do. Forgiveness proves to you and others that you are larger than the circumstances that sometimes befall you. And that will magnetize people all the more to your leadership.

summary

KEY POINTS TO REMEMBER

- Forgiveness is the final and conclusive step in transforming the anger that harms your relationships and blocks your power.

- Forgiveness is a gift you give to others, but which you especially give to yourself. It benefits you more than the forgiven.

- Forgiveness demonstrates to others just how powerful you are. It demonstrates that you are larger than your anger and larger than the offenses directed at you.

ACTIONS TO ENHANCE YOUR POWER

- Ask yourself, "Whom have I been angry at for a long time? Whom have I not forgiven?" Reflect on how your anger is harming you and blocking your passion. If you are then ready to forgive, first put your forgiveness in writing for your eyes only. As a next step, decide whether and how to communicate it. If you are not yet ready to forgive, consider writing a note to yourself: "I hope and intend to get to a point where I am ready to forgive."

IF YOU CHOOSE TO EXPRESS
YOUR ANGER, DO SO CONSCIOUSLY
AND SKILLFULLY

In some instances, it may be necessary for you to express your anger before transforming it. In such cases, be careful to act consciously and without blame. So if you wish to express your anger directly at the person who has offended you, be certain that your language is emotionally neutral. Otherwise, you will likely trigger negative reactions that could harm you and your relationship. For similar reasons, consider understating your anger and buffering your message with positive statements about your colleague and your connection. So acting will ensure a more productive conversation.

Sometimes, you may first have to voice your anger and grievances before releasing them. In situations where this is true for you, express yourself as necessary. But be thoughtful in how you do so.

First of all, check to ensure that you are not about to blame the person you are preparing to speak to. It is very rare for blame to be an effective relationship or leadership tool. Generally, people will not be willing to accept your blame and instead, they will resent you. And as discussed earlier in this chapter, you will be giving away responsibility, and therefore your power, to the very person you are blaming.

Also, assuming you wish to enhance your relationship with the person to whom you are speaking, try to be as emotionally neutral as possible. Simply state, in effect, "This was your action and this is the impact it had on me." If your words are attacking or laced with anger, then only more anger will come back at you. For this reason, it is usually wise to delay before giving a voice to your anger. If, for example, you wait 24 hours, you will likely be much less emotionally activated.

Also consider understating your anger. Then it will be easier for the person who has offended you to listen. It is very distressing for people to hear that they've triggered anger in

the very person standing right in front of them. In such a case, they will typically feel vulnerable, fearful, and ashamed. Then they may also get angry themselves. So if you are irritated with the person, it is often enough to say something like, "I'm feeling a little frustrated." The listener will amplify the intensity of your statement anyway. If you make your words much stronger, you may trigger an emotional chain reaction in him that will be difficult for either one of you to control.

Finally, consider providing an emotional buffer for your statements. Say something positive that helps your colleague withstand the negative and not slip into a defensive pattern. For example, you might say, "Although what you did upset me, I like you and I respect you." Or you might say, "I'm telling you about this because I so value our relationship and I don't want anything to get in its way." Of course, you would only say such things with great sincerity and only if they were true.

KEY POINTS TO REMEMBER

- If you wish to express your anger at the person who has provoked you, consider using the following approaches to avoid undue harm to your relationship:

  - Ensure that you are not blaming him.

  - Be as emotionally neutral as possible.

  - Understate your anger, as he will likely amplify it anyway.

  - Use an emotional buffer of positive statements to help him tolerate your communication.

ACTIONS TO ENHANCE YOUR POWER

- Review two or three instances in which you expressed your anger at others. What were the results? Consider whether the outcomes may have been better had you been more emotionally neutral in your statements, and had provided a positive emotional buffer. If you find you would have likely achieved better results with these approaches, consider using them in the future.

6

TRANSFORM YOUR DISCONNECTION INTO RELATEDNESS

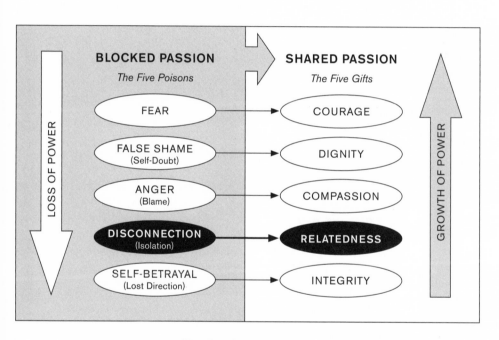

The Five Gifts Roadmap

OBSERVE YOUR DISCONNECTION SO
THAT YOU CAN TRANSFORM IT

| Observe Your Disconnection | Listen Mindfully | Speak Openly. | Give Generously |

When you linger in your anger, fear, and false shame, you will naturally descend into a state of disconnection from other people. Superficially, you may still maintain the appearance of a relationship, but really, you will be closed off and there will be a wall around you. Yet, to be a powerful person and leader, you need others' help and support. And they will not fully provide it if they don't feel a solid connection with you. People want your attention and want you to take an interest in them. When you provide them these gifts and choose to be continuously connected, you will have greater power.

Do you, like most leaders, sometimes get disconnected from those around you? To the extent you do, notice how that harms you. How many of your goals can you accomplish alone, without the sincere efforts of others? People are not likely to wholeheartedly support you unless they feel a connection with you.

Examine closely, then, the quality of your relations with the people you look to for help and support. Do you really know them? Do they truly know you? And how much, honestly, do you care about them? Your answers to these questions will show you how much these people care about you—and to what extent they really *want* to help you. You can make your requests and your demands—and then get angry when people fail to deliver. But a wiser and more powerful course is to consider what you can actually expect based on the connections you have nurtured.

If this is not making complete sense to you, reflect on the times when others wanted a lot from you. Were you so willing to make sacrifices when not feeling a solid connection with them?

The previous three chapters followed the downward path on the Five Gifts Roadmap, covering fear, false shame, and then anger. One reason these emotions are so harmful is that if you stay in them, then almost certainly you will descend into the next poison, disconnection. You will disconnect from others and perhaps even from yourself. We'll discuss the first type of disconnection in this chapter and the second type in the next. Keep this crucial point in mind: When you are cut off from others and from yourself, you are cut off from your power.

Most often, it is anger and resentment that causes you to disengage from people. That's why disconnection directly follows anger on the Five Gifts Roadmap. But your fear and your false shame drive a wedge between you and others, too.

I consulted to an executive who would get very disappointed in his colleagues and angrily write off his relationships with them. "I'm not going to waste my time with those people," he'd say. But it was his hurt and anger, clearly visible to anyone who would look, that were making these decisions for him. And he actually needed the people he was shunning.

Is this how you sometimes react to your disappointments, too? Perhaps your response is not as dramatic, but don't you pull back from people when you feel let down by them? Consider how many relationships you have lost as a result—and how that may have harmed you. You have more empowering options available to you.

Or perhaps it is more your insecurities than your disappointments and anger that keep you from others. Do you feel inadequate around some people and therefore avoid them? Are there events you do not attend and organizations you do not join because you feel self-doubt in comparison with those who will be present? Isolating yourself in front of your computer or TV might help you temporarily avoid these feelings. But it is actually making you weaker. It is your connections with others that will build your confidence, provide you support, and enhance your power.

A former classmate of mine is a brilliant business strategist and highly valuable in the services she renders. Yet, several times she complained to me that others within her company contributed much less than she but earned far more. "Could it be," I finally asked her, "that they have built stronger relationships than you?" She was silent for a moment and then told me how lonely she was growing up as an only child with parents distracted by their own careers. As a little girl, she would even follow the postman from door to door, desperate for some attention. And then finally there came a point when she gave up on people. "I know I should be doing more networking," she said, "but sometimes I just don't feel very confident. Sometimes, it just feels safer inside my cubicle."

Small cubicles in large organizations are filled with such people. Have you ever wondered whether, at least to some degree, you may be like them? Could you be more successful by building relationships with more

> **DEEPER WISDOM**
>
> People sometimes say, "It's not what you know, but who you know." Although there is much truth in this, it is often said with some cynicism and even envy—as if your access to relationships were beyond your control. That perspective can make you feel powerlessness and tempt you to be passive. A more powerful stance is to acknowledge the importance of relationships and then to proceed with building them using the tools provided in this chapter.

people? In the sections that follow, I'll give you the tools for doing so. You may have noticed that those who enjoy the greatest success are often not the most talented. Rather, they are the most connected.

You may actually be very connected with a number of individuals. But as you look at yourself closely, can you see there are other people, whole groups of them, you entirely wall out? They may be those in a different part of your organization. Or they may dress differently or look differently than you or have a different political ideology than yours. Likely, it is your fear, anger, or false shame that is causing you to be closed to them. We human beings naturally want to connect when those feelings are not present.

In organizations, this disconnection generates inefficiencies and much conflict. And your choices can have even more far-reaching effects. When you distance yourself from people—in your work environment, your family, and your community—they will likely sense it and feel hurt and dishonored. And that will activate their feelings of inadequacy and resentment. Consider how these results of your actions endanger you.

So ask yourself, "Who am I not connecting with? What feelings does this create within them and within me? Is my distance really protecting me—or is it harming me?"

Every time you disconnect, you also miss out on the positive experience you could have generated. Do you notice that you feel better about yourself when you are more connected to others? Your energies and your passion actually need interpersonal contact to be most activated. And when you are more connected to people, they will feel better about you. They are wired to need your acknowledgment and attention. So they will appreciate your efforts when you show some interest in them—or even when you simply smile at them. In these ways, you can continuously leave behind a trail of good feelings and good will. This will only benefit you.

> **POWER TALK (to self)**
>
> - "Who am I disconnected from?"
> - "What are they feeling about me as a result?"
> - "Could my disconnection be harming me?"

Pay attention, then, to your degree of connection with the people around you. Do you have any sense of their thoughts and feelings? Of what they most need and desire? How often do you speak to them to truly get to know them? You can take steps now to be more connected—and more powerful.

summary

KEY POINTS TO REMEMBER

- When you are feeling angry, fearful, or inadequate, it is natural that you will disconnect from people. Likely, you often do this to some degree.

- Your disconnection harms you. As a person and especially as a leader, you need people's support. Almost certainly, you cannot accomplish your goals alone. Yet, when people do not feel a solid connection with you, they will not truly support you.

- Your disconnection from others can also cause them to feel hurt, inadequate, and angry. These feelings may be strong or they may be more subtle. Either way, they create further dangers for you.

- Consider instead continuously strengthening your links with other people. Likely, you will find that the quality of your relationships, at least as much as the degree of your talent, determines your level of success.

ACTIONS TO ENHANCE YOUR POWER

- Make a list of all the people whose support you need in your work, ranking them from 1 to 5 in terms of their importance to you. Using the same 1-to-5 scale, also rank the quality of your relationships with each of these individuals. Ideally, the importance ranking you give each person will be at least matched by the relationship quality ranking. Any gaps, especially regarding those whose support is vital for you, will indicate where you most need to build better connections.

- After you have completed the above exercise for your professional life, consider using it for your familial life and other social relationships. Avoid the temptation to be dismissive of certain people and their importance for you. Be impeccably truthful with yourself instead. You may find some significant opportunities you can address while that option is still available to you.

LISTEN MINDFULLY AND WITH CURIOSITY

Your disconnection from others results from not seeing them for who they truly are. The remedy, then, is listening to them mindfully and with curiosity. Tune in to their perceptions and their experience including, especially, their experience of you. You will probably find that your disconnection from them is matched by their distancing from you—and, quite possibly, their related negative emotions. Likely, they will not communicate those feelings directly to you. But they will do so in indirect ways, which you can hear if you listen closely and with compassion and empathy. To ensure a better connection, also ask questions that show your genuine interest. Then summarize what you hear to confirm your understanding. Initially, you may not want to hear all this information available to you. But it is vital for your relationships and greatly empowers you.

Your disconnection is based on beliefs and judgments about others that are likely incomplete and just not true. Getting more connected, then, requires setting aside those perceptions and getting curious about the people around you. As you truly listen to them, your beliefs about them will become more accurate and complete. Seeing people for who they really are, you will be much less inclined to withdraw and disconnect. To the extent, instead, that you are not openly listening, you will be trapped inside your habitual, even reflexive, ways of seeing.

It will actually be easier for you to remain disconnected. Based on your negative emotions, you may justify this by thinking, "It's no use talking with those people." Or, "They're not worth my time." Such thoughts may be loud and strident within you, or they may be subtler. Look out for them and when you see them, consider how they are affecting you. Are you using them to comfort yourself and to stay safely distant and apart? Aren't these justifications telling you that you're powerless to better unite with other people?

I once encountered a senior leader in a large and complex organization who would typically force through his initiatives. He wasn't known for his patience or listening abilities, but was known for his brilliant marketing savvy—and for usually getting his way. "They want to have these long meetings," he explained, "but I think they're a waste. After a while, either they get it or they don't. Either they're with me or they're against me." About one year later, when I spoke with him again, he seemed more sober. There was a move afoot in the organization to strip him of some key responsibilities. He had few allies to call on.

As we sat at a table together, assessing the damage, he bent forward, rubbed his forehead with his fingertips, and recalled a time when he was a boy. His family's whole house was shaking as his father nailed two-by-fours across the inside of the front door. They were meant to prevent his older brother from returning. His father had just thrown him out. The next day, this executive recalled, there were new locks on the doors. "I wonder," he said, "if I'm kind of like my father. I wonder if I've been kind of shutting out my sons and my brothers. And maybe that's been really hurting me."

When my client changed course and started listening, he was disturbed by what he heard. He found that most people did not quite understand what he had been doing. And more important, he also came to realize that his style had been triggering their feelings of inadequacy and therefore their ire. His approach was so threatening, their opposition was actually just an expression of their self-protection.

Could you be shutting out others, too? Try stepping away from your judgments about them and from your preoccupation with how they affect you and instead try listening with care. Rather than indulging your normal human propensity to think so much about yourself, think about them. Say to yourself, "I wonder what this person's experience is. I wonder how she sees things." Even more powerfully, ponder, "I wonder how this person experiences me." Listen intently—and then see the additional knowledge and power this provides you. You may be surprised by what you discover.

> **POWER TALK (to self)**
>
> - "I wonder how this person sees things."
> - "I wonder how she experiences me."

Like my client who faced much opposition, you may learn that the people you've disconnected from are actually having negative reactions to you. Your withdrawal from them may have been preceded by their defensive distancing from you. Or it may be your disconnection itself that has triggered their negative emotions. Either way, listen to these individuals with sensitivity. Listen for the fear, anger, or false shame that is likely driving them. Probably, they will not tell you about their negative reactions directly. But if you listen for the indirect communication of their grievances, you will likely find what is triggering them.

A CEO had a strained relationship with a key member of his team. He wanted to improve matters, so he invited her to dinner. He told me afterward, though, that this hadn't made their relationship any better. "What did you talk about?" I asked. "She talked a lot about her father," he replied. He seemed annoyed. "What did she say about her father?" I inquired. "A lot of things about him being critical and demanding and it being hard to please him." "I think," I said, "she is talking about you." I explained she was likely unaware for the most part that she was even doing so.

"But I'm not really critical and demanding," he retorted. I suggested, though, that he ask her a few questions designed to get at the truth of the matter. Her answers ultimately revealed that she was, in fact, experiencing him as terribly unfair and oppressive. Once he made a few adjustments in his approach, their relationship became much better.

As was true in this case, people will sometimes communicate their unhappiness with you by talking about another person who upsets them rather than talking about you. Sometimes, they're secretly hoping you get the message. More often, they are not even aware of their motive. Or if they are more deliberate, they may ask you a question such as, "Am I giving you everything you need?" Or they may say, "Call me whenever you need me." They are coaching you on how they want you to interact with them. If you're not listening carefully, you will miss the message and further damage your connection.

To get more connected to others, then, listen very carefully so that you get the indirect messages they are sending you. Especially in professional settings, most people are not comfortable directly telling you their negative reactions. So don't just listen to their words, but "listen" as well to their facial expressions, to their eyes, and to their bodily postures. In my training to be a psychologist, a supervisor once told me, "Dean, if only you would listen, *really* listen, you will be amazed at what you hear."

But often, you may not want to listen—because if you do, you may hear things about the other person and about yourself that are upsetting. You may hear that your colleague—or your spouse or other family member—is quite angry with you. You may discover that you have hurt her badly. You may learn that she feels tormented by you. You will hear all sorts of things and some of them will disturb you. Yet, it is your knowledge of these very matters that enables you to connect more fully and be more effective. Your knowledge is indeed the source of your power.

The usual pattern, though, is to not listen and to stay, to some degree, comfortably disconnected. This is why my clients are almost always surprised when I show them the results of my interviews with their colleagues. Before I work with them, they typically believe they know how others experience them. But as they discover, their knowledge had been lacking. Like most leaders, they hadn't been mindfully listening. And that caused disconnection and a leakage of their power.

To listen most effectively, do so with compassion. Remind yourself that just like you, the people you shun have their struggles, their worries, and their insecurities. Just like you, they are doing the best that they can.

And listen with empathy too. That will help you go beyond your limited perceptions and truly understand the person in front of you. By imagining what he is feeling and letting yourself feel some of those emotions too, you will gain valuable insights. As a result, you will be far more effective—and more powerful—in your interactions. So in your listening, ask yourself, "What would cause him to see things this way? What is he feeling?"

Your connection will also be enhanced when you ask some questions. And your queries will be most effective when they demonstrate your genuine interest and invite meaningful disclosures. So you might ask, for example, "How do you see this issue?" Or, "What's your perspective?" And you might ask, "What do you think we should do?"

Try to resist the natural inclination to present your point of view first. People really don't want to listen to you until they feel you have truly listened to them. So instead of starting your conversation with the tone of, "Let me show you how right I am," start with the spirit of, "I want to hear your point of view."

Once the person has spoken, summarize what she has said. Reflect back the points that you sense are important to her and confirm you have heard her emotions as well. But bear in mind that although most people want their negative emotions recognized to some degree, they are not comfortable when those feelings are acknowledged to their full extent. This is especially true in a professional context. Accordingly, soften your acknowledgment of the speaker's emotions. If he is furious, it is sufficient to affirm that he is "frustrated" or "annoyed." If the speaker is very afraid, it is often enough to acknowledge that she is "concerned" or "kind of worried."

And once you have completed your summary, ask, "Did I get it right?" In doing so, you demonstrate it is important to you to understand your colleague. And half the time, she will correct you. So by checking for accuracy, you ensure a more complete understanding and a better connection.

Consider making it your habit, then, to carefully listen to others. Likely, you will be surprised by what you discover. The knowledge you gain will strengthen your relationships and will enhance your power.

KEY POINTS TO REMEMBER

- Your disconnection from others is the direct result of beliefs and judgments about them that are incomplete and largely not true.

- To remedy your disconnection, it is therefore necessary to correct and fill out your understanding of those around you. You can do so by listening to them mindfully and with curiosity.

- Your disconnection from some people will often be matched by their withdrawal from you. Likely, they will also have some negative feelings toward you. They may only communicate these feelings indirectly, such as by speaking of others who upset them. Or they may "speak" to you through their posture and facial expression.

- You may not want to hear some of what your colleagues have to say as it may be upsetting. But understanding their perspectives is the basis for your connection and is therefore essential for your power. So listen attentively and with compassion and empathy.

- To get people talking, ask questions in a way that demonstrates your genuine interest in their perspectives. Then summarize what you have heard and check for understanding.

ACTIONS TO ENHANCE YOUR POWER

- Identify three people who satisfy both of these criteria: (a) You have at least partly disconnected from them due to your negative judgments; and (b) having a closer relationship with them would enhance your effectiveness, success, or life satisfaction. Spend at least 15 minutes with each of these individuals, closely listening to them. Ask questions to show you are truly interested in what they have to say and then summarize what you have heard. Challenge yourself to set aside all your judgments and to listen with compassion and empathy. Afterward, record what you have learned about each person, including their emotional states. See if you can use this information to experience them differently, be more open to them, and have better relationships with them.

SPEAK OPENLY AND AUTHENTICALLY

| Observe Your Disconnection | Listen Mindfully | Speak Openly | Give Generously |

To get reconnected with others and stay connected, speak your truth. Do so openly and boldly, revealing not just your thinking, but also your feelings and your hopes and desires. Of course, use appropriate discretion and focus more on your positive than negative emotions. Typically, the more you reveal of yourself, the more people will have something to "plug into" and the more they will trust you. You may feel less exposed and safer if you are more withdrawn and quieter, but then you would be letting your fear and false shame govern your actions. As you make efforts to get better connected, you may find that you had earlier triggered people's negative reactions. In such cases, acknowledge your behavior patterns that contributed to the problem and commit to changing for the better. More broadly, consider developing ways of concisely telling others about yourself so they can more quickly and accurately know you.

To transform your disconnection from others, speak to them openly and authentically. Extend yourself outward and speak your truth. Tell people your thoughts, your beliefs, and your perspectives. And especially, reveal your feelings and your related hopes and desires. When you are so self-revealing, a stronger connection will naturally follow.

One of the people who taught me the most about connecting powerfully was not a business executive with immense resources at his disposal. Rather, he was a teenager in a simple white T-shirt and jeans who approached me at a bus stop in a poor Oakland, California, neighborhood in 1983. I was 24 years old, having just arrived from New York and a bit hardened by a number of years of urban living. As he began to ask me for something, I tuned him out, looked away, and said I had no money.

But this young man needed to be heard. He insisted, "Look at me." I looked up, we made eye contact, and he stated, "I'm not asking you for money. I'm just asking that when the bus comes, you get a transfer and put it out the window. Then I'll take the next bus." I silently nodded while I heard the roar of the approaching bus. I boarded and he stayed on the bench. As I requested the paper transfer, I did not worry about whether I was about to violate some ordinance or rule. I was moved by the simplicity and power of this person's direct statement of his need.

What happened next on that nearly empty bus is etched in my memory as a still and silent moment—my hand pushing through the small, cramped space of the bus window opening; the driver looking up, peering at me through his rearview mirror; the elderly, heavy woman in the front seat turning to observe disapprovingly; the little wisp of paper that was the transfer dancing in the breeze of the bus's wake; and the young man I had just met, running alongside the bus, his arm outstretched, reaching for the transfer. I think he actually caught it.

Could you also speak so clearly and directly from your heart and ask for what you really want and need? Could you gently insist that people truly see you? When you speak your truth like this, you cut through the layers of people's defenses, studied avoidances, and polite refusals—and you enhance your power.

It is through your emotions that people will most see you and *feel* you and have a clearer sense of you. So long as your emotions are appropriately modulated and not targeted against them, people will generally welcome learning more about you. However, to ensure your colleague's receptivity, focus your self-disclosures more on your positive emotions rather than the negative ones. To create even more connection, show these positive feelings—such as your excitement, enthusiasm, and caring—in your vocal tone, facial expressions, and postures. And consider tying all this in to what you and your colleague can accomplish together. As you help others feel more connected with you, you will naturally feel more connected with them.

Yet, many people limit themselves as they relate to others. For example, has someone ever spoken to you whom you found dry and boring? Likely, she was not revealing her feelings and related desires. More to the point, have you ever noticed yourself talking and still not feeling connected? In those instances, you were probably also keeping your emotions and dreams sequestered.

Restricting your disclosures may help you feel less exposed and safer. But by limiting your connections, you are actually putting yourself in danger. And you are allowing your conduct to be driven by your fear and false shame. So consider taking more risks and being more self-revealing. It is your feelings and aspirations that will draw people closer to you. If, on the other hand, you just speak about facts and logic, most people won't feel a strong connection.

I once observed an executive seem "fake" in a meeting with her colleagues. I had an unsettled feeling in my gut as I watched her. She appeared like a corporate automaton, functioning mechanically in her role, even smiling at the appropriate times, but seemingly devoid of any human warmth and feeling.

She was very different in our following interaction, so I stated my experience of her then as warm and easy to talk to. I asked her, though, if she experienced herself any differently in the meeting that had just transpired. She acknowledged that she had been more "professional" in that context and that, actually, she felt she had to act this way in business settings.

I told her I had noticed the difference. I suggested that in business, she was coming across as inauthentic and that this was likely making people uncomfortable. She was surprised but wasn't seeing any other option. She was equating the business world with a certain degree of superficiality. Not surprisingly, her work relationships were suffering and people did not completely trust her.

This executive was a little extreme, but might you also sometimes appear to others as a bit contrived? Or, more likely, as a bit too distant and "professional"? When you experiment with speaking more openly and authentically, as my client learned to do, you will likely have some pleasant surprises. You will find that people welcome your genuine self-disclosures. Once they understand you better, their trust in you will be greater.

Consider revealing, even, some of the challenges within your own personality. When you do, people will be relieved that you have struggles like they do. Then they will feel more of a kinship with you. You are more powerful when you own and accept all of yourself, including your vulnerabilities, and show that to other people. Being so open, you are demonstrating that you are not hobbled by self-doubt. You are boldly doing what most others are afraid to do. And your openness implicitly gives others permission to be open with you.

To speak about yourself and your thoughts and feelings, consider starting in a way that prepares the listener. For example, you might say, "Let me tell you what's happening with me." And then, when you speak, be certain to do so compassionately and sensitively. See if you can relate your statements to what you know about the other person and his emotions. When you can say, "I have the same concern" or "I've been frustrated as well" or "I feel the same as you," then you build a bridge of emotional commonality between the two of you.

> **POWER TALK (to others)**
>
> - "Let me tell you what's happening with me."
> - "I have the same concern."
> - "I feel the same as you."

> **A**CKNOWLEDGMENT. Openly acknowledging your conduct that has upset the listener and damaged your relationship.
>
> **I**MPACT. Explicitly recognizing the impact of your conduct on him—and on the relationship.
>
> **C**OMMITMENT. Committing to change the behavior in question.
>
> **F**EEDBACK. Asking for ongoing feedback to help ensure the change in behavior.

FIGURE 6.1 AICF Relationship Enhancement Tool

If the person you want to reconnect with is upset with you, then consider the following approach that will resolve most of those feelings. A colleague used a version of it with me some years ago when our relationship was quite strained. She could be abrasive at times and one day sarcastically criticized me in front of a group of people. She had done similar things in the past and I was unhappy with her conduct. Yet she took a countermeasure the next morning that astonished me.

She walked right up to me, looked me in the eye, apologized, and then went further. She said, "I realize I have a caustic streak in my personality and that you probably find it offensive. I don't like it myself and I want you to know I'm working hard to change it. Please tell me if you ever see me acting that way again." My anger all but vanished right there in the moment.

This approach worked so well partly because my colleague was so open and authentic with me. She was confident and powerful in making her statements, yet also quite vulnerable. But the vulnerability only made her stronger and more effective.

Let's look at the elements of this approach so that you can use it, too. I call it *AICF*—an acronym for Acknowledgment, Impact, Commitment, and Feedback. It is summarized in Figure 6.1.

The first step is *acknowledgment*. This means openly acknowledging to the other person—your boss, peer, spouse, friend, or any other person important to you—your conduct that has upset him and potentially harmed your relationship. If the conduct is part of a larger pattern, it is helpful to acknowledge this as well.

The next step is *impact*. This means explicitly recognizing the impact of your behavior on the other person, on your relationship, or both. For example, you might say, "I realize it frustrates you that I tend to dismiss your ideas." Or you might say, "I recognize that my habit of criticizing you gets in the way of our having a better relationship."

Next is *commitment*. This is where you state your resolve to change your behavior. You could say, for example, similar to my colleague, "I'm going to really try to change this." It is even more powerful, though, to state your unequivocal commitment to change. Consider simply saying, "I am *committed* to changing this."

The final step is *feedback*. Here, you ask the other person to tell you whenever she observes you returning to your old behavioral pattern. You might say, for example, "Please tell me whenever you notice me doing this again." But bear in mind that even if they agree, most people will be reluctant to actually volunteer such information in the future. Therefore, at a couple of subsequent points, reiterate your desire for the feedback. In these ways, you confirm that you are committed to changing and that you indeed value the relationship.

For every one of your relationships that has some strain and distance, consider using this four-step approach. This assumes that your conduct has contributed to the problem. Very likely, that's the case. Almost all difficulties in professional, familial, and social relationships are co-created. Naturally, you may

> **DEEPER WISDOM**
>
> When you repeatedly engage in a behavior that is upsetting for a colleague or family member, you create a power imbalance where the other person feels powerless to change your conduct. But when you commit to changing your behavior *and* ask for ongoing feedback about it, you restore a balance of power in the relationship. Your colleague or family member will then feel empowered to speak out about the behavior that upsets him and insist on its correction. With this balance of power restored, he will be far more willing to invest in the relationship.

want to blame the other person. But if you let that stop you from taking corrective action and insist that she "go first," nothing will likely happen. The most powerful thing you can do in such a situation is to take responsibility yourself for improving the connection.

Better than telling people about challenging aspects of your personality after difficulties arise is telling them beforehand. In this way, you proactively manage the relationship. For example, if you like to probe and test people's thinking as I've noticed many CEOs do, consider advising them in advance. And explain why you do so. You might say, for example, "I have a tendency to challenge people's ideas and I'll probably do that with you. It's my way of testing input and making sure we're coming up with the best solutions." Having prepared the listener, you are less likely to later trigger her false shame reactions.

More broadly, just as businesses are clear about their brand and "messaging," be clear about your own. For example, as you are getting to know people, you might tell them, "There are three things you should know about me." Then list them. Try to make them positive, such as "I'm very excited about . . ." or "I deeply care about . . ." The more authentic and heartfelt these statements are, the more impactful they will be.

> **POWER TALK (to others)**
>
> - "There are two things you should know about me . . ."
> - "Here's what you can expect from me . . ."
> - "Here's what I'm about . . ."

Even more powerfully, consider telling people what they can actually expect from you. Then enumerate two, three, or four items. Make them succinct, powerful, and authentic. For example, you might say, "I'm tenacious and won't give up until we get to our goals" or "I'll be there for you." This is a confident, compelling, and memorable way of introducing yourself and helping others better know you.

As you reveal more of yourself openly and authentically, you will feel more connected. And you will be helping others feel more connected with you. It is not withholding and silence, but self-disclosure that typically renders you most powerful.

KEY POINTS TO REMEMBER

- To effectively transform your disconnection from other people, extend yourself to them and speak openly and authentically with them.

- Reveal your thinking and beliefs, and to create a stronger connection, also reveal your feelings and aspirations. So long as you keep the expression of your emotions appropriate and largely positive, people will typically want to hear them.

- As you increasingly reveal yourself, others will feel they more know you and will therefore more trust you. It may feel safer to be quieter instead, but limiting your relationships actually puts you in greater danger.

- When you want to resolve your distance from a person who is upset with you, openly acknowledge your conduct that helped cause the problem. Next, explicitly recognize the impact of that conduct on him and on your connection. Finally, commit to changing and ask for feedback moving forward.

- Just as companies are thoughtful and clear about their messaging, it can benefit you to do this, too. Consider developing concise and authentic ways of describing who you are as a person and as a leader.

ACTIONS TO ENHANCE YOUR POWER

- Identify three relationships that you want to be closer but that are currently somewhat distant. These may involve the same three people you identified for the exercise at the end of the previous section. For each of these individuals, identify two to four items you could disclose about yourself that would likely build more of a connection. For example, you might reveal a positive feeling you have about the person or about a project or goal that you share. Or you might talk about your family or an interest or hobby. Give yourself several weeks to gradually share all this information. It's best to start with the items that are easier for you. With practice, you will get more comfortable disclosing the information that feels more challenging. Afterward, assess your connection with each of the three individuals involved. Evaluate to what extent you are now closer.

GIVE GENEROUSLY, FOR PEOPLE NEED
WHAT YOU CAN PROVIDE THEM

Your most powerful solution for transforming your disconnection is to give generously to others. Especially give to meet people's twin needs for recognition and caring. So let the essence of your giving be, "I see and appreciate you, and I care about you." When you fill such vital emotional needs for people, you become more important to them. You may notice that many of your own resentments and frustrations result from not having these same needs met by others. But instead of focusing on what you want, focus on what you can give. When you give the very thing you desire, you are more powerful. And people will naturally want to give back to you. But don't give with expectations as that will dilute your gifts and undermine them. Instead, give with pure emotional generosity. Then watch and see what flows back to you.

One of the most powerful things you can do is to give—and to do so generously. It helps immeasurably in transforming your disconnection and building your relationships. It affirms your bond with other people. Giving material things can be very important, but assuming that people's basic physical needs are satisfied, it is the giving of your attention, care, and concern that will resonate most strongly. When you give to people on this emotional level, you are feeding many of their deepest needs and desires.

A manager at a food company told me one way her CEO showed his care for the employees. One morning, she arrived early and found him on his hands and knees, sweeping up the trash around her cubicle with his hands. He seemed, she said, to be without any trace of self-consciousness as he went about the task. He simply looked up and said, "This isn't right that you folks haven't been getting any help with this." There had been a problem with the janitorial service, so he had taken it upon himself to tidy up. "There he was," she recounted, "a 63-year-old man, all six-foot-four and 220 pounds of him, our CEO, picking up *my* trash. I felt such a strong urge to throw myself down on the floor alongside him and do my part. And I did."

So when you notice you are disconnected to some degree from another person, reach out to him and see what you can give him. Give your earnest attention. Show a genuine interest in his thoughts and opinions. To the extent you can do so appropriately and truthfully, compliment him on his abilities. Help him feel good about himself and his value. You might say, for example, "I see you're good at this" or "I appreciate you." And consider showing that you care about him as well. It can be very powerful for you to ask, with deep sincerity, "How can I help you?" or to simply say, "I like you."

> **POWER TALK (to others)**
>
> - "You're good at this."
> - "I appreciate all that you do."
> - "I like you."

These forms of emotional giving are so potent because people need them so deeply. Actually, nearly all people have a twin set of powerful emotional needs. The first is for recognition and acknowledgment of their value. The second is for caring. You can know the importance of these needs by consulting your own experience. Would you want to work with someone who really didn't care about you? Or who didn't show she valued you?

Yet, so often, these needs are poorly satisfied, including among leaders. When you personally meet such crucial needs for others, you become very important to them. So keep this paradigm in mind in your encounters with acquaintances and colleagues: "I *see* you. And I *care* about you." Then try to put it into action.

People are so hungry for this emotional nourishment that they will be magnetized to you to receive it. And in the giving, you will be ever more enriched. It is as if you have entered an impoverished village and have a caravan of camels with you as long as the eye can see, laden down with food. When people are hungry, feed them. Especially consider this when it costs you so little and benefits you and others so greatly.

> **definition**
>
> **EMOTIONAL GENEROSITY**
> Giving to people to help meet their emotional needs—including their need to be seen and appreciated and their need for caring.

So for every relationship that is important for you and for every disconnection you want to transform, simply ask yourself, "Does she feel *seen* by me? And does she feel I *care* about her?" This is about your *emotional generosity*. And that largely determines the quality of your connections.

I consulted to a vice president of research and development who had left a teaching post at a top university for his current role. A prolific researcher, he had been irritated with the "sluggishness" and administrative obstacles of academia and had hoped for a faster-paced environment in the business world. Yet his frustration now was at least as intense as before. His many technical insights were so brilliant and revolutionary, his colleagues could barely comprehend them. Therefore, he was not getting the support he needed.

The crux of the problem, I told him, was his lack of emotional generosity. I suggested that others were experiencing him as "the mad scientist," but he could choose to be "the kindly professor" instead. As the former, he was alienated and angry. But as the latter, he could patiently provide explanations to his colleagues and welcome their input. In these ways, he could help them feel capable and valued rather than inadequate and insignificant.

He seemed open to this perspective, but I had not anticipated the extent to which he'd embrace it. He actually started a "university" within the company and even spent considerable amounts of his personal time recruiting instructors for it. But it was his own courses, he said with a twinge of modest embarrassment, that were the most popular. He explained, "There is something rewarding about

teaching that I'd almost forgotten. It feels good to give something to others." When I asked about his frustrations with his colleagues, he laughed and said, "That seems like a long time ago."

How about you? How emotionally generous are you choosing to be? And what impact is that having on your relationships? What impact is it having on your power?

We talked about listening and speaking in the previous two sections. When you listen and speak in ways that meet people's emotional needs, your interactions will be all the more effective. When you listen to your colleagues attentively and with genuine interest, they will feel seen by you and they will feel your care as well. And as you speak through your words and your actions, you can also provide your colleagues the recognition, appreciation, and care that they desire.

As we have discussed people's needs for recognition and caring, have you thought about how well those needs are met, or not met, for you? Perhaps, like most people, you have some frustrations and resentments regarding what others are failing to provide you. But when do you feel more powerful—when you are waiting to receive something from others or when you are giving it to them? Consider choosing to give the very things you wish to receive. Then observe the impact on your power.

So identify what you want from others. Do you want greater loyalty from those you lead? Then provide that loyalty to them. Do you want your people to care more and be more engaged with their work? Then care more about them and be more engaged with them, too. Do you want your family members and friends to be more sensitive to your needs? Then be this way with them.

When you give to people, they will feel grateful and will *want* to give back to you. Think of your own experiences with those who have been very generous with you. Haven't you wanted to return some of that generosity to them?

For your giving to be powerful, though, it must be done without expectations. If you expect or strongly desire to get something back in return, your motivation will likely be detected. And then your gift will be substantially diluted. In such cases, you risk coming across as insincere and manipulative. You may end up undermining your connection rather than enhancing it. The paradox is that the less you expect back, the more you are likely to receive.

Your challenge, then, is to give to others based on pure generosity. Let the gifts of your attention, care, and concern come from a desire to help people feel better about themselves and better know their value. Let your gifts flow from your wanting people to know that others care. Then watch and see what happens. At the very least, you will feel better about *yourself* and *your* value. You will also feel a stronger connection. And the recipients of your gifts will likely want a greater connection with you.

So consider expanding your emotional generosity. It can deepen and expand your connections immeasurably. And it will feel good for you. By giving rather than seeking, you greatly enhance your power.

KEY POINTS TO REMEMBER

- To resolve your disconnection from others, give to them. Especially give to meet their twin, powerful needs for recognition and caring. Let the essence of your giving be, "I see and appreciate you, and I care about you."

- Demonstrating such emotional generosity is one of the most powerful things you can do. By meeting people's vital emotional needs, you magnify your importance for them and solidify your connection.

- Like many people, you may have frustrations and resentments about others' not meeting these needs for you. Your more powerful stance, though, is to give what you wish to receive. When you do so, people will naturally want to give back to you.

- But be careful to not give with expectations of receiving as that will likely be detected. That can taint your giving and render it less meaningful for others. Instead, let your gifts flow from a natural generosity. Then observe the positive results that come back to you.

ACTIONS TO ENHANCE YOUR POWER

- For the next week, perform three acts of emotional generosity every day, beyond anything you normally do. Focus your efforts on people with whom you want to build a stronger connection. Especially attend to their twin needs for recognition of their value and for caring. Be genuine, offer something meaningful, and expect nothing in return. Then record the results of each interaction. Note the impact on the other person, on you, and on the connection.

- Identify two or three of your emotional needs that are not being fulfilled adequately. They will likely be variants of the needs for recognition and caring. Write out the needs in words that are most meaningful for you. Then, in regard to each need, provide to others the very thing you want on at least five separate occasions. To make your giving an even richer experience for you, do it with the people you feel are withholding these very things from you. This can be a very powerful exercise, so take your time with it—but do it diligently. Then observe its impact on others—and on your power.

7

TRANSFORM YOUR
SELF-BETRAYAL INTO INTEGRITY

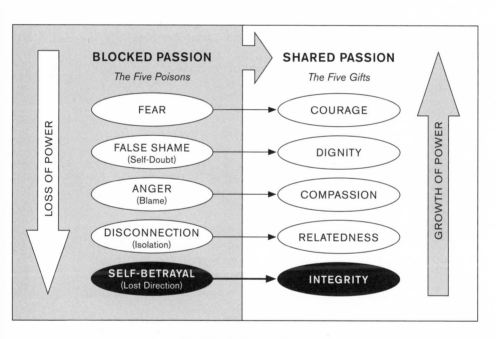

The Five Gifts Roadmap

BE AWARE OF HOW YOU LOSE YOURSELF

Be Aware	Commit to Your Values and Mission	Manage Your Emotions	Prioritize Internal Success

The last step down on the Five Gifts Roadmap is self-betrayal. At that point, you betray what feels right and deeply true for you. You may do work not meaningful for you or say or do things contrary to your values. Acting in these ways undermines your self-esteem and self-trust and greatly limits your power. It's called self-betrayal because these acts first dishonor you. Then they dishonor other people. But by transforming your self-betrayal into integrity, you can be whole again and reclaim your power. The first step in this transformation is seeing your self-betrayal plainly and clearly. By looking with compassion instead of judgment, you will see more and proceed more quickly.

Look inside and see if you can find instances of acting inconsistently with your deeper truths and values. Examine your conduct with resolute honesty, yet proceed compassionately because your looking may not be easy. Like most people, you'll probably discover you sometimes betray what is most important to you. When you betray yourself in these ways, you are betraying your power.

For example, do you have a sense of greater goals you could be pursuing in your life's work but that you ignore and set aside? Do you instead engage in other activities that are not meaningful for you and that do not fulfill you? Do you ever say to yourself, "Why am I doing this?" or "Why do I stay in this situation?"

Or, rather than being longer-term, some of your self-betrayals may be in the moment and situational. For example, do you ever say things, or do things, out of your fear, impatience, or anger that you regret later? In such cases, you may say to yourself, with exasperation, "There I go again!" Or you may ask, "Why did I do that?" One government official, reflecting on his past lapses, told me, "Deep down, I don't trust myself. I've hurt a lot of people."

Self-betrayal is acting inconsistently with what feels right and deeply true for you. So acting from time to time is common among people, but it depletes your power and harms you. And on a broader scale, to the extent you have allowed your work, or your life, to be smaller and not reflective of who you actually are, the result is a profound loss of your power. This would be most apparent if you were to say, "I hate my job" or "I hate this part of my life." But you betray yourself as well when you say, "My heart's not really in it" or "This doesn't feel right for me," yet you do that very thing nonetheless.

> **definition**
>
> **SELF-BETRAYAL**
> Acting inconsistently with what feels right and deeply true for you. This often includes violating your principles and values.

When you act in ways that betray your truth, you will naturally feel badly and your self-esteem will suffer. Your self-betrayals also undermine your ability to trust yourself. And if you can't trust yourself, how can you expect others to trust you? You may sometimes think these compromises you make render you safer, more secure, or more effective, or otherwise provide you some advantage. But when you're not true to yourself—when you *lose* yourself—what do you have left? Any self-betrayal is actually a great threat to your power.

In some of the leaders I've worked with, I've found that deep within, their current situations were making them terribly unhappy. They even felt as if parts of themselves were dying. They had been afraid to acknowledge this to themselves, let alone to others. But when I reflected back to them what I saw, they recognized what I was seeing. Sometimes, the problem was they were in a role not right for them. At other times, it was something different.

In either case, they realized they had been out of balance and ignoring their fundamental truths and deeper needs. Driven by their fears and insecurities, they had been neglecting essential parts of their lives. For example, they may have been disregarding intrinsic talents or abandoning personally meaningful activities. They may not have been spending enough time with their spouses and children. Or they might have bypassed a path for their development that was, in fact, crucial for them.

How about you? In what ways are you not true to yourself? When you are aware of how you lose yourself, then you can transform that self-betrayal into integrity. That will restore and deepen your power.

In organizational life, you will often feel pressures to silence your truth. But doing so can actually imperil you. One CEO I encountered disdainfully referred to some of his executives as "kiss-asses." He said, "I don't want them to tell me what they think I want to hear. I want them to tell me what they really see and believe." In other words, he wanted his executives to be in integrity.

You may think of integrity in the more typical sense—as abiding by certain moral or ethical standards. But more deeply, it means being whole and undivided. The essence of integrity is acting in a way that is true to yourself—such that there is only one of you and you're moving in one direction. When a business or any other organization is not unified and all moving in the same direction, it is likely to suffer greatly. The same is true for you.

Therefore, a loss of integrity is first and foremost a wrong you do against yourself. That is why I call it self-betrayal. First, you are not true to yourself and lose your direction. Then what naturally follows is betrayal and harming of others. You must first dishonor yourself before you dishonor other people.

For example, you may know of leaders who profess values of treating people, such as their employees, fairly and respectfully. But when feeling stressed, they treat others in discourteous and even demeaning ways. First, such leaders betray their values and their vision of the leaders they intend to be. And then they betray others.

Do you, like most people, get critical of others who fall out of integrity and act unethically? Any such judging and blaming will interfere with understanding how your colleague, friend, or partner came to that point. And it will impair you in identifying your own gaps in integrity and more clearly understanding them. As with the other poisons, the best course for resolving self-betrayal is not judgment, but compassion.

To the extent you betray yourself in ways large or small, it's because of your fears, insecurities, and resentments. That's why self-betrayal is the final step down on the Five Gifts Roadmap. That descent starts with the poisons of fear, false shame, and anger. When you fall into them and stay there, you make yourself vulnerable to betraying what is most dear to you. And when you disconnect from others, you deprive yourself of the protection from self-destructive choices that strong social ties provide you.

DEEPER WISDOM

One of the reasons why people tend to judge others' losses of integrity so harshly—especially when they involve violations of moral, ethical, or legal rules—is that they fear, deep down, that they could act similarly. Your judgments of others, therefore, may relate to your judgments against yourself. When you develop a more compassionate and understanding approach toward yourself, you will likely start treating others the same way. In this manner, you can develop more effective relationships both with yourself and with other people.

Your challenge, then, is coming home to your true self and therefore to your integrity. Your integrity is indeed an essential source of your power. And if you listen carefully, your integrity will guide you in making the changes it requires. But you don't need to start making changes in your life abruptly and immediately. Instead, consider taking just one small step at a time. Moving at this pace may be more sustainable as you gradually take back your power.

Your first step, though, is earnest self-awareness. See how you are not being true to yourself and how you therefore deplete your power. Then you can change course using the approaches I'll now show you.

summary

KEY POINTS TO REMEMBER

- You betray yourself when you act in ways contrary to what feels right and deeply true for you. For example, you may violate your principles and values. Or you may engage in activities that are not meaningful for you, to the exclusion of other endeavors that could fulfill you.

- By acting in such ways, you undermine your self-esteem, dishonor yourself, and greatly deplete your power. This is why it's called self-betrayal. First you betray yourself. Then, as a result, you will typically betray other people.

- Self-betrayal is the final step down on the Five Gifts Roadmap. It therefore arises from negative emotions and from your disconnection from other people.

- You can transform your self-betrayal into integrity. The first step is clearly seeing how you have lost yourself. You will see more and proceed more quickly when you look at yourself with compassion rather than with judgment.

ACTIONS TO ENHANCE YOUR POWER

- Set aside 30 to 45 minutes where you can be alone in a comfortable place. Take two minutes to breathe slowly and deeply. Relax as much as possible. Then read the following questions and see which one(s) most resonate for you or feel most fitting for you. And then choose those questions to answer. To make this exercise most effective for you, be compassionate with yourself throughout its duration.

  - "What larger goals of mine have I been disregarding?"

  - "What do I do—and not do—that disappoints me about myself?"

  - "How am I not true to myself?"

  Once you have your answers, organize them in order of "least difficult for me to change" to "most difficult." Using the approaches in this chapter and, as relevant, those throughout this book, start addressing these integrity challenges one by one. It is probably best if you start with the least difficult one and then address successively harder ones. Addressing all the items on your list may take many years and may still not be possible. Being true to yourself is not a black-and-white issue. Rather, it is a matter of degree—and it is a lifelong challenge.

SOLIDIFY YOUR COMMITMENTS TO YOUR VALUES AND YOUR MISSION

Be Aware → **Commit to Your Values and Mission** → Manage Your Emotions → Prioritize Internal Success

The next step in transforming your self-betrayal is determining your values and mission and resolutely committing to them. Doing so will provide you a strong and precise inner-guidance system. That will keep you whole and unified, continually moving in one direction. To take this next step, look deep inside, identify the values and larger goals most important to you, and commit to these very things. Continuously strengthen those commitments by monitoring your conduct to ensure that you are acting consistently with them. Consider telling others your mission and values, too. By taking these actions, you will deepen your commitments to yourself—as well as your commitments to other people. That will enhance others' trust in you. And it will also enhance your power.

To strengthen your integrity and guard against self-betrayal, identify your values and mission. And then fully commit to them. Make these commitments an oath that binds you. When you make them that strong, they will consistently and clearly guide you. Being so unified within yourself as you move forward, you will observe that your presence and your leadership will become a force of greater power. And naturally, you will more magnetize others.

Do you notice, though, as you consider making these commitments, that you feel a certain reluctance to do so? That is only natural. But instead of avoiding this task and missing out on the power that such commitments can provide you, ask yourself what holds you back from taking this step forward.

Are you concerned you don't quite know your values and mission and therefore aren't sure what to commit to? I will show you how to identify these guiding lights that are likely already within you. Are you fearful you may not be able to adhere to your commitments once you make them? It is true you may fall down at times on your path, but then you can pick yourself up again. And that is better than having no direction to start with. More deeply, are you concerned that you may lose some of your freedom? That is inherent in any commitment, but consider whether, compared with the loss, your gain will be even greater.

When you are prepared to make these commitments, start with your values. Once you have clearly listed them, you can act more consistently with them. When they are only implicit, you are more at risk of violating them and thereby undermining your confidence and your power. And when you can clearly state your values, this helps you in your relations with others.

At a meeting I attended some time ago, someone asked a senior executive, "What are your values as a leader?" He looked at his shoes and said, "I don't know." Judging by the silence that followed, his response undermined his stature as a leader. Perhaps it also rendered him less trustworthy in the eyes of others. If he didn't know the values that guided his behavior, how could he be counted on to do the right thing?

Actually, I saw this leader as very values-driven in his actions. But he hadn't taken the time and effort to ascertain his values so that he could articulate them to others.

To create a set of committed values for yourself, start by identifying the three to ten values that most speak to you. These would be the core and fundamental guidelines you endeavor to live by, your personal code of honor. Ask yourself, "What do I stand for?" Or more concretely, ask, "What behavior do I expect from myself?" Then record your answers.

To make your list of values most meaningful, consider recording them as "I will" statements. For example, your values might include, "I will treat others with respect and fairness." Or, "I will not let my fear and anger govern my actions." To make your values even more absolute, add the words *always* and *never*. For example, "I will always be true to my word." Or you might say, "I will always hold my power and never diminish myself."

Keep in mind that your values will not just be commitments to yourself. They will also be commitments to other people. Therefore, in identifying your values, reflect on how you want to show up for the people important to you. Then state your values accordingly. For example, one value might be, "I will continuously share my knowledge with my colleagues." And another may be, "I will always be there for my wife and children."

Once you have created your list of values, expressly commit to them. Speak your commitment out loud to yourself or put it in writing. Then keep your values in a place easily accessible to you and review them often. At such times, ask yourself, "Am I being true to my commitments?" Then be rigorously honest in your answers.

Consider using your list of values proactively and not just reactively. So when you are facing a major decision that has ethical or interpersonal implications, pull out your values list and see what guidance it provides you. Use them as well if you are struggling in a relationship with a colleague, family member, or friend. Rather than blaming the other person, consult your values to formulate a plan for interacting that preserves your dignity and your power.

Consider also, at select and appropriate times, stating your values to others—even when they don't ask about them. Consider saying, for example, "Here's what I stand for . . ." or "Here's what I'm about . . ." Then speak your values, and do so with great sincerity. This deepens your commitment to them and helps people to better trust you.

> **POWER TALK (to others)**
>
> - "Here's what I'm about."
> - "I'm committed to always acting in this way."

Once you have identified and committed to your values, your next step is determining and committing to your mission. Define your mission in terms of your professional life or broaden it to apply to your life overall. Your mission is your purpose. It is what, in the larger sense, you are setting out to accomplish.

If you haven't identified your mission and are pondering whether to do so, ask yourself some questions. For example, are you able, without a clear mission, to keep yourself moving in one direction? Might you be expending vast amounts of time and energy

> **definition**
>
> **MISSION**
> Your larger purpose in your work or in your life overall. The greater goal you desire to accomplish.

attempting to move in multiple directions that don't feel right, and actually aren't right, for you? And if you lack an explicit mission for your professional activities, might that signify—to you and to others—that you are not fully committed? If you're not so committed to your work, can you expect your colleagues to be so committed in their support of you?

You may have various short-term and medium-term goals, but as such, they are not permanent. When they shift, they cause you to shift, too. A mission provides you a greater goal—a purpose—that stays constant and continuously guides you. Your values show you how to act along your path, while your mission shows you where you are going.

For many people, having a mission assumes there is something they have been "called" to do. But if that terminology doesn't work for you, ask yourself instead, "What am I meant to do?" Or, "What will most fulfill me?" Or look back on your life and ask, "When was I most fulfilled? When did I experience the deepest satisfaction?" Imagine, even, lying on your deathbed and looking back on your life from that perspective. In so looking, what accomplishment will provide you the greatest satisfaction and your life the greatest meaning?

> **POWER TALK (to self)**
>
> • "What is my purpose in my work and in my life?"
>
> • "What will most fulfill me?"

As you consider these questions, allow them to percolate within and let your mission emerge for you. Open yourself to the range of possibilities. A friend who did this exercise told me, "My mission in life is to give guidance to the next generation so they can be the best people they are capable of being." Another leader I know simply and boldly wrote, "My mission is to cure cancer."

Part of my own mission in life is to provide people insight and understanding that helps heal the world and relieve its suffering. Once I identified my mission, I dropped some professional activities that had been unsatisfying and that, previously, I had been too afraid to leave. With all my energies focused, laser-like, in one direction, I became more effective. Being in deeper integrity, I also grew more content and peaceful.

Once you have identified your mission, put it in writing and commit to it. And commit it to memory as well. Then notice how your activities compare with your commitment. Probably not everything you do will directly support your mission. Necessarily, some of your daily activities will only indirectly support it. Be on the lookout, though, for work that distracts you and even undermines your purpose. When you become aware of such conduct, ask yourself if it might be a form of self-betrayal.

Just as you may communicate your values, consider doing the same with your mission. Your colleagues will better understand you when they know what most drives you. But be careful not to let your mission sound like mere advertising. Just as with your values, speak of it only with utmost sincerity.

Once you identify your values and mission and commit to them, you will be a more cohesive and powerful force. And as you continuously live by these commitments, you will become ever more unified and trustworthy in your efforts. Your greater success will naturally follow.

summary

KEY POINTS TO REMEMBER

- To protect yourself against self-betrayal and to enhance your integrity, identify your values and mission and definitively commit to them. These commitments will provide you clear guidance and will keep you moving in one consistent direction.

- Your mission is your larger purpose or destination. Your values are the principles for your conduct as you move in that direction. To identify your values and mission, look deep within and find what is of greatest importance to you.

- Once you have identified your values and mission and have committed to them, put them in writing and review them often. The truer you are to your commitments, the greater your power.

- Also consider telling others about your values and mission. This will enhance people's trust in you, especially if you are earnest and heartfelt in the telling.

ACTIONS TO ENHANCE YOUR POWER

- First, identify your *values.* The relevant instructions are included in the text above. In summary, identify the three to ten principles for your conduct that feel most important for you. These are the fundamental guidelines you live by. You can identify more than ten of them, but to the extent you do so, you risk creating a list of values that is diluted and more difficult for you to keep in mind. Once you have identified your values, record them and commit to them. To make your values more powerful and meaningful for you, consider writing them in the form of "I will" statements. For example, a value might be, "I will treat people with respect and kindness." Once you have a set of committed values, do the following:

- At the end of each day during the next week, evaluate your conduct against your values. For now, simply notice the discrepancies. The exercise at the end of the next section in this chapter will provide you additional steps for addressing them.

- As you monitor your conduct, also notice anything you do that doesn't feel quite right for you, but that does not violate your stated values. Consider supplementing your values to cover this conduct as well.

■ Next, identify your *mission.* Consult the relevant instructions in the text for doing so. In brief, this requires you to determine the larger purpose in your work or in your life overall. To help identify it, ask yourself one or more of the following questions: "What will give my work or my life the greatest meaning and satisfaction?" "What will most fulfill me?" "What, in the past, has most fulfilled me?" "When have I experienced the deepest satisfaction?" After you have identified your mission, record it and commit to it. Then do the following:

- Identify an action you can take in the next three days that brings you one step closer to fulfilling your mission. Make the step as small as it needs to be to ensure that you actually take it within the set timeframe. The important matter at this point is not the size of the step, but that you are moving.

- Once you have completed the first step, follow the same procedure to take the second one. Do the same for the third step and so on. Keep moving forward.

MANAGE YOUR EMOTIONS TO CHOOSE
THE MOST POWERFUL ACTIONS

A lack of integrity in someone is not due to their being a "bad" person. It's due to emotions that have risen up and taken control of them. So look closely, and you will likely see it is your fear, anger, and self-doubt that typically cause you to violate your own values and lose your direction. To stay in integrity, then, be on the lookout for your negative emotions and continuously manage them rather than letting them manage you. Be especially alert when you find yourself saying, or thinking, that you have no choice but to take certain actions. That's typically a false claim of powerlessness fueled by your emotions. And it's a danger signal that you are about to fall into a state of self-betrayal.

When you find you have betrayed yourself, trace back your steps on the Five Gifts Roadmap. See if you can identify which negative emotions you have succumbed to that caused you to forsake your values and lose your direction. It's even better, though, if you can catch these emotions before they harm you. Managing your emotions, then, is essential to maintaining your integrity and holding your power.

Have you noticed, though, how some people choose to *not* hold their power? Have you heard people say, "She made me do it"? Or, "He provoked me"? Sometimes, it's more subtle: "I had no choice"; "I had to do it." Have you ever said such things yourself? Or thought such things? These attempted justifications are actually self-statements of powerlessness. They tell you that you have no power when actually you do. When you surrender control in this manner, you will soon skid into a state of self-betrayal.

Look behind the feelings of powerlessness and likely you will find your negative emotions. You may believe you haven't made a choice, but hasn't your fear, anger, or false shame dictated the choice for you? These feelings can make you believe you have no power. But nearly always, you have the ability to choose an action that is best for you.

For example, let's say you're staying in a desperate situation in your work that betrays your mission and torments you. You feel you have no choice, but is that really true? What fears and self-doubts are blocking you? Or you violate your values by erupting with impatience at your colleague—or at your child. Before claiming your reaction was only natural, and before labeling the other person's conduct that triggered you, look inward and see how you, in that moment, surrendered control to your emotions and thereby forfeited your power.

Look more broadly and consider the extent to which you are sometimes different depending on the emotions swirling within you. In the eyes of others, how many versions of you are there? And if you are not consistently in control of yourself, how much, do you think, are people willing to trust you? Generally, people want to see only one of you, not different personalities that show up depending on the unpredictable flow of your feelings.

Effectively managing your emotions takes a combination of self-awareness and self-mastery. First, you must be aware of the negative emotions that are present. Next, your challenge is to master those emotions and not let them dictate your actions. This is true self-possession. We discussed self-possession in Chapter 5. It means that you, not your emotions, are in control. With such control, you are more likely to stay in integrity and not relinquish your power.

To enhance your self-awareness and therefore your integrity, know how each of the first three poisons—fear, false shame, and anger—can trigger your self-betrayal. For example, when you are trapped in your fear, you are more likely to take desperate action not true to yourself and your commitments. When you are angry, you are more likely to rashly say things and do things you may regret later. And when you are immersed in false shame and feel badly about yourself, you are more likely to do things that harm your self-esteem further. In such a state, you are also more likely to get angry and then act unwisely.

So be on alert and observe yourself continuously and carefully. Notice when you are not being true to your values. At such times, pull out the Five Gifts Roadmap and determine which negative emotion—fear, anger, or false shame—has led you astray. Then turn to the chapter for transforming that emotion and follow the instructions for taking back your power.

> ### DEEPER WISDOM
>
> Many leaders attempt to enforce a sense of integrity in themselves and others by establishing rules and prohibitions. But rules and various "shoulds" can be of limited use when people get taken over by their negative emotions. Therefore, one of the most powerful things a leader can do to enhance integrity in her organization is to create a positive emotional climate. This helps prevent destructive emotions from arising in the first place. The initial step, then, is the leader managing her own negative emotions lest they spread to others around her.

Also notice when you are not being true to your mission. Identify the negative emotions that here, too, have taken you off course. Then make the necessary corrections to get yourself moving again in the right direction. Your fear and self-doubt will likely grow stronger as you proceed in spite of them. But rather than giving in to these emotions, keep moving forward. As you do so, your fear and self-doubt will ultimately recede, and you will reclaim your integrity and power.

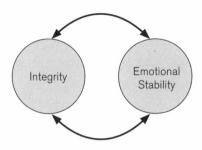

FIGURE 7.1 The Virtuous Cycle of Integrity and Emotional Stability

Perhaps managing your emotions and staying true to yourself does not normally seem too great a challenge for you. But what if you are under great stress and things are not going well for you? What if the whole world seems to be crashing down around your head? Consider these times as great opportunities to exercise and grow your integrity and your power. Then challenge yourself to move forward calmly and decisively despite the fears, self-doubt, and resentments that may be bubbling within you.

When you are true to yourself and your commitments, those commitments will become stronger. And you will feel better about yourself, and your dignity will grow greater. Overall, you will be building up the strength inside of you. As a result, you will be less destabilized by events that would otherwise disturb you. In this way, your integrity increases your stability. And your emotional stability—your consistent management of your emotions—enhances your integrity. As shown in Figure 7.1, your integrity and emotional stability therefore feed each other in a virtuous cycle.

So when circumstances threaten your commitments to your mission and values, when your fear, anger, and self-doubt threaten to engulf you, be aware of what is happening inside you and choose to manage your emotions. Choose to hold your power. Ask yourself, "What is the most powerful choice I can make right now?" Then take whatever action your answer provides you.

POWER TALK (to self)

- "Are my emotions eclipsing my values?"

- "What is the most powerful choice I can make right now?"

KEY POINTS TO REMEMBER

- When you violate your values and act contrary to your mission, it's typically because you are letting your fear, false shame, or anger guide your actions. So by carefully managing these emotions, you can protect your integrity and guard against self-betrayal.

- Your acts of self-betrayal are often preceded by thoughts or statements that you have no choice in your conduct. These attempted justifications are, in reality, false assertions of powerlessness. And they are driven by your fear, self-doubt, and resentments.

- Integrity and emotional stability each enhance the other. When you increase your integrity, you will feel better about yourself, you will feel stronger, and you will be more emotionally stable. And when you are more emotionally stable—more in control of your emotions—you will have greater integrity. This is a virtuous cycle that empowers you.

ACTIONS TO ENHANCE YOUR POWER

- In the first exercise at the end of the prior section, you identified your values and monitored your compliance with them. If your values are sufficiently challenging, you have likely noticed at least subtle violations of them. See if you can identify the negative emotions that have triggered these self-betrayals. Record not just the relevant emotions, but also the overall patterns by which they cause you to go astray. This will equip you for better anticipating and guarding against these emotions in the future.

- In the second exercise at the end of the prior section, you identified your mission and started taking steps to more fully implement it. Reflect back on those steps and carefully observe yourself as you take additional ones. What emotional states are arising as you move forward? Keep a log of them. Notice how they continuously shift. And most important, don't let them determine your actions. Instead, continue simply taking one step after the other.

PRIORITIZE INTERNAL SUCCESS— AND EXTERNAL SUCCESS WILL FOLLOW

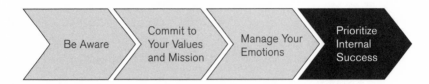

Like most leaders, you may be primarily focused on external success—matters outside yourself over which you have only limited control. If so, you are vulnerable to feeling powerless and ultimately falling into self-betrayal. To be more powerful, prioritize your internal *success. Focus, then, on your integrity, over which you have complete control. Accordingly, continuously measure the extent to which you are staying true to yourself and your values and are not capitulating to your negative emotions. When you so attend to and honor your integrity, it will grow ever stronger. Paradoxically, by being less preoccupied with external success, you will find it flows more readily to you. Even in those instances in which it temporarily eludes you, you will have preserved and fortified your power. And then you will be more equipped for harvesting other successes in the future.*

As the final step for transforming your self-betrayal, prioritize your integrity. Continuously assess the extent, therefore, to which you have remained true to yourself and your values. Assess whether you have not let fear, anger, and false shame govern your actions. When you measure yourself in these ways, you are measuring your internal success and therefore your internal power. And because you are measuring these qualities, they will tend to change in the desired direction. You will become stronger, more steadfast, and more solid. And people will more trust you.

But most people focus more on *external*, rather than *internal*, success. Do you do that, too? If so, you are depleting your power. You are mostly evaluating yourself based on events outside of you—like business results—that you cannot fully control. Over time, the outcomes of such events will necessarily vary. When they are favorable for you, your self-worth will increase. And when these outcomes are negative instead, then your self-esteem, and your overall state, will turn negative, too. You will be poised to tumble down into self-betrayal.

Rather than letting your self-worth and emotional states ride up and down based on events outside of you, consider anchoring yourself with your integrity. Consider asking, from time to time, "Am I being true to myself? Am I not letting myself be governed by fear, anger, and false shame?" You cannot completely control the circumstances external to you, but you can control your internal states and how, therefore, you show up as a person and as a leader. When your primary measure is your own integrity rather than your business success, you have greater power.

> **POWER TALK (to self)**
>
> - "Am I being true to myself?"
> - "Am I in control rather than my fear, anger, and false shame?"

Imagine a leader more focused on each quarter's business results than anything else. Her emotions are positive for now because current events in her business happen to be positive, too. Envision another leader who takes her business goals very seriously, but whose primary yardstick is staying true to herself and her values. Therefore, her business results and day-to-day successes and failures do not determine her self-worth. And they have only a limited impact on her emotions.

Of the two, who is the more powerful leader? Who is more likely to stay the course and remain self-possessed when events—as is bound to happen—start exploding unpredictably around her? Who is more likely to be a rock of stability for others? Who is more likely, then, to constellate the trust and commitment of colleagues and customers?

Now take a moment and examine yourself more closely. Which of these two types of leaders are you more like? Do you get dejected when the successes you want in your work, or in your life, don't happen? Do you then get irritable and testy? Or anxious? Or start feeling inadequate and unworthy? These emotions arise from evaluating yourself based on events you are powerless to control completely. When you measure yourself in these ways, you only torment yourself and deplete your power.

What if, instead, you were to primarily evaluate yourself on matters that, right now, you *can* control? What if you were to assess yourself based on your integrity—on your adherence to your mission and values, on your acting in ways that felt right and true for you? Consider how that would affect your power. Consider how it would affect your emotional states that could otherwise push you into desperate acts of self-betrayal.

Once you have prioritized your integrity, you can still wholeheartedly pursue the goals with which you have been entrusted as a leader. In fact, your integrity will typically require you to do so. And you will be more likely to achieve those objectives. When you are true to yourself, you will have greater energy and passion. And the force of your outward efforts will be counterbalanced by your calmness, steadiness, and adherence to your values. Operating from that core of inner strength, you will be more likely to realize your goal's completion.

The paradox, then, is that when you are less obsessed and frenzied in your pursuit of external success, it will come more easily to you. Unfazed by obstacles and events that disappoint and frustrate others, you will have an inner power that attracts success—and that attracts others.

Regardless, you will not always be successful in your outward efforts and will sometimes have failures. But how do you want to experience them? If you have given fully of yourself, yet acted with composure, you will feel the disappointment of your losses, but not the chagrin and disquiet of having failed to hold your power. When you have honorably played your part, you can still feel good about yourself despite the outcome. As a business leader I know once said to me, after suffering a near-catastrophic failure, "Dean, I don't like the result. But I like the way I showed up."

> **POWER TALK (to self)**
>
> • "I don't like the result. But I like the way I showed up."

After some months or years, your memories of particular outcomes will fade and many of them will no longer seem important. But the memories of how you acted will remain with you and with other people too. This will determine how you feel about yourself and how others feel about you—and respond to you—for years to come. So what will live on is the accretion you made to your power—or the depletion of it that you allowed instead.

When you assess yourself on your integrity, though, remember to be kind and compassionate with yourself. And forgive yourself for your errors. If, instead, you berate yourself for your mistakes, you will undermine your self-confidence and drain your passion. If any punishment is required for your self-betrayals, the consequences that naturally arise are punishment enough. You need not punish yourself further through harsh self-criticism that only harms you.

So to transform your self-betrayal, continually measure your actions against your integrity. Do so diligently, yet kindly. Remember that as an imperfect person, you cannot help but make errors. As you proceed in this manner, your integrity will grow—and so will your power.

summary

KEY POINTS TO REMEMBER

- The final step for transforming your self-betrayal is prioritizing your *internal* success and therefore your integrity. Your integrity is a matter over which you have complete control. Therefore, by focusing on it and continually measuring it, you can substantially enhance it.

- Consider, then, making your *internal* success, rather than your *external success,* the primary measure of your worth. You have only limited control over events external to you, such as your business results. So when you rely on such matters to determine your self-esteem, you risk feeling powerless and falling into self-betrayal.

- Focusing on your integrity will still support your energized commitment to your external goals. In fact, it will render you more capable of attaining them. Operating from the inner core of calm and stable strength that integrity provides, your accomplishments will flow more readily to you. And you will more magnetize the trust and support of other people.

- You may not always reach your external goals. But when you honor your integrity and therefore stay true to yourself and your values, you will feel good about yourself despite your outcomes. And after the memories of your various successes and failures have faded, you and others will still remember how you showed up as a person and as a leader.

- Because you're an imperfect person, your actions will sometimes be inconsistent with your integrity. But when you err, be kind and compassionate with yourself, and forgive yourself, too. So acting will protect your self-esteem and render you more likely to uphold your integrity in the future.

ACTIONS TO ENHANCE YOUR POWER

- Identify one goal you have, the attainment of which is not completely under your control, but which you feel you "must" or "have to" accomplish. Notice the fear, anxiety, and other negative emotions you are likely feeling as a result. Notice also the sense of powerlessness this situation generates within you. Then try this experiment: Tell yourself that even more important than this goal is holding your internal power and staying absolutely true to yourself and your values. Know that *no one* can take that away from you. Imagine, then, not reaching your goal, but still feeling strong in your integrity. Notice how that impacts your emotional state and your experience of your objective. You may discover an inner core of quiet strength that guides you with less torment and greater ease to your goal's actual completion.

8

· THE POWER OF PASSION ·
RELEASE POTENT ENERGIES
TO LIFT YOU AND YOUR LEADERSHIP
TO HIGHER LEVELS

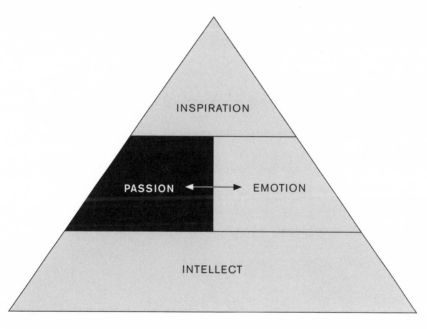

The Four Powers Pyramid

ENSURE YOUR PASSION IS AN AUTHENTIC
EXPRESSION OF YOU AND YOUR DEEPEST DESIRES

To enhance the life energy and vitality that is your passion, first identify and transform the negative emotions that likely block it. Then, when you are ready, take additional steps to make the flame of your passion even brighter. Get fully connected with yourself and your deepest desires. And focus your energies on what most stimulates and excites you. In so doing, you will move beyond everyday integrity into the realm of heightened passion and a deeper authenticity. This will be confirmed by the energy you'll feel swelling within you. Be ever alert, though, that you not misuse your energies to express your negative emotions—or to avoid them. That only dishonors you and creates false passion. True passion, on the other hand, always expresses your authentic self and your deeper desires.

Passion is your life energy. It is your vigor and vitality. It is the very means by which you make your efforts and make things happen. And your own passion activates the passion in others so that they join with you most fully. Therefore, the flow of your passion is crucial for you.

You are already born with an abundance of passion. You can develop even more of it with the approaches I will now show you. But do not make that your primary focus as it is not likely your primary challenge. Rather, if you are like most people, the *blockage* of your passion is the major problem.

Therefore, the single most powerful set of actions you can take to heighten your passion is to identify and transform the poisons on the Five Gifts Roadmap that block it. Chapters 3 through 7 provide you the necessary instructions. So to free up the flow of your passion, you must be adept in managing your negative emotions. Recall that is why passion and emotion sit side by side in the Four Powers Pyramid with an arrow between them.

Once you are doing all you can to master your emotions and un-block your passion, follow the guidance in this chapter to make the force of your passion even greater. As an initial step, check to ensure that you are connected to yourself and your deepest desires. We already discussed being true to yourself in the previous chapter. But now, take your integrity one step further. Integrity can feel more like the "push" of what you should do. Passion is more about the "pull" of what you most ardently desire such that in your actions, you are truly enthused and excited.

To be stimulated to this degree, you must be fully connected with yourself. You must know what makes you content and happy. Some years ago, I worked with an older business leader in Asia who seemed to me quite wooden. I told her, "I sense you have blocked passion." She was startled and then acknowledged, "That's my problem. I've really lost my passion." She then relaxed into her chair and began to tell me about her life as a young girl. She would spend hours sitting in the *kampung*—the village—silently watching the palm tree leaves rustle in the wind. As she spoke, she seemed more alive and happy.

I asked her, "Can you go back to the kampung? Can you go back and watch the palms move in the breeze?" I explained that when she did this in the past, she connected with an essential and powerful part of herself that she still very much needed. She liked the idea and found a way to once again be among the palms whenever she felt the need. And then, over the following months, we witnessed the gradual reawakening of her joy and her passion.

To activate the deepest reserves of your passion, you must know yourself and your profoundest desires. You must also focus on what most stimulates you. Ask yourself, therefore, "What do I most deeply want to do?" This may involve using your unique gifts and skills in a profession. Or you may have a dream to develop a talent, to write a book, or to mentor young men or young women. You will know you have touched your passion when you begin to feel its energy surging within you.

To live your passion, don't be overly influenced by what others do or tell you, for they may have deadened their passion, too. Instead, listen to the voice deep within and honor it. Give yourself over to what most speaks to you. Unfold and flower as you were meant to. Then you will give your greatest gifts and be most powerful. This is beyond everyday integrity. This is the realm of pure authenticity. The flow of your energy that results will be the natural flow of your passion—and it will feel good for you.

Be careful, though, that your passion not get contaminated by your negative emotions. For example, do you become irate and even infuriated by what seems unjust and unfair to you? Do you then get "passionate" about rectifying those matters? Being energized by your anger is not true passion. As you will soon see as you read further, passion is about your connections with others. Anger, on the other hand, cleaves people apart.

When you act in anger, you feed it and push yourself deeper down into the poisons of the Five Gifts Roadmap. And your actions will likely be divisive, off-putting, and ineffective. Energy and passion, like emotions, are contagious. So your angry outpourings of energy are likely to activate similar attacks by your opponents. Do you think that's the most effective way of proceeding?

Ensure, then, that the focus of your passion is "for" people rather than "against" them. And ensure that your passion is an authentic expression of the deeper you rather than an expression of negative emotions that have temporarily seized hold of you.

Therefore, also beware of making "passionate" efforts actually driven by your fear and false shame. Such efforts may superficially appear passionate and you may believe them to be so. But your passion then is actually false. When your fear and self-doubt are dictating your actions, you are not expressing your deeper self and deeper desires. Rather, you are merely reacting to negative emotions that, in the moment, you have succumbed to. It is only when you work your way back to the gifts side of the Five Gifts Roadmap that you can begin to express the true passion that pulsates within you.

Instead of using your passion to express your negative emotions, you might use it to avoid them. This, too, is false passion. So you may devote your energy to projects and activities to distract you from certain emotions you'd rather not feel. In such situations, you may actually believe you are "passionate." But question whether you are truly expressing the deeper and authentic parts of you. And consider whether, by ignoring your emotions, you are disregarding some crucial information they are trying to provide you.

A former attorney who had been working 70-hour weeks told me, "I used to complain about all the work, but it actually provided me a convenient way of being so busy that I didn't have to deal with my feelings." But then, as always happens, his hidden unhappiness caught

> **DEEPER WISDOM**
>
> When people devote extreme amounts of energy to their work, they are sometimes avoiding problems in their home life and marriage. The "passion" at work that results will then be unbalanced and unstable. And their marriage and family will deteriorate further. To avoid this scenario, continually check in with yourself using the Five Gifts Roadmap. When you are effectively managing the five poisons, you will not misuse your passion in ways that harm you and other people.

up with him. Only then could he start looking at his life and making some meaningful changes. "I was in a lot of pain back then," he said, "but I just didn't know it."

So be mindful of how you use your energies. Putting them in the service of expressing or avoiding your negative emotions is not true passion. And such a misuse of your energies dishonors and harms you. Ensure that your passion is instead always in the service of authentic self-expression. That will keep your passion flowing most strongly.

summary

KEY POINTS TO REMEMBER

- Passion is your life energy and vitality. You are born with it in abundance, but it typically gets blocked by your negative emotions. Therefore, your first step in enhancing the flow of your passion is to identify and transform the poisons on the Five Gifts Roadmap that obstruct it.

- You can increase the power of your passion even further by getting more fully connected with yourself and your deepest desires. By focusing on what most stimulates and excites you, you can move beyond everyday integrity into the realm of a deeper authenticity and a greater passion. You will know you have activated that degree of your passion when you begin to feel its energy surging within you.

- Be careful about diverting your energies into either expressing or avoiding your negative emotions. The resulting activities may superficially appear passionate, but they will likely be ineffective. You will only be showing a false passion—and a dissipation of your power.

ACTIONS TO ENHANCE YOUR POWER

- Identify at least several instances in recent years when the efforts you were devoting to your work or other activities were substantially greater than what is typical for you. For each such instance, assess the nature of your engagement. In which ones was your true passion indeed flowing? In which, instead, were you merely expressing or avoiding your negative emotions? Notice the differences between these two types of experiences. This will better equip you to make wise choices for the use of your energies in the future.

- Set aside a half-hour to be in a quiet place. Sit comfortably and relax. After a few minutes of breathing quietly, ask yourself what you wish to do in your professional life that would *truly* stimulate and excite you at the deepest levels. Do not label anything as unfeasible or unrealistic. Do not censor yourself. Instead, let your imagination expand freely. Notice the emotions that arise as you do this exercise—both the positive emotions and the negative ones too. Notice how your energy levels are affected as well. Then record your findings. Once you have gained sufficient mastery over the five poisons that would otherwise obstruct you, consider incrementally moving toward the realization of your work-related desires that so excite you.

PUT YOUR POWER IN THE SERVICE OF LOVE
TO GENERATE THE GREATEST PASSION

In both your personal, intimate life and your public work life, your passion is the same fundamental life energy. And when it's an expression of your love, it will rise to its greatest level. Of course, how your love and passion emerge in the different parts of your life will vary. In work, your love will be evident in your care, interest, and concern. It will be evident in how you give to other people. Power without love is brittle and sterile. But if you choose to put your power in the service of love, it will generate passion at the highest level.

True passion is not solitary and self-focused. And it involves more than authentically expressing yourself and your deepest desires. In fact, true passion is also an expression of your love for other people. So consider putting your energies in the service of love. Then your passion will surge to its greatest levels.

This may seem most apparent to you for romantic relationships. And you may view the passion of your intimate life as very different from the passion of your work. Certainly, the expression of passion in these two domains is different. Yet in both your personal life and your work life, passion is the same basic energy. It is the fundamental life energy that flows through you. And that energy flows most powerfully when it's an expression of your love for other people.

In your work, think of love as your genuine care, interest, and concern. And think of it in terms of what you can give to others. How passionate do you think you can be as a leader when there is no love in your efforts? And when you are not giving your gifts? See if you can find within yourself a deeper caring that fuels your endeavors.

If it seems odd to you to genuinely care about your coworkers, consider the number of hours you're with each other. Consider the months or even years you have toiled together. And consider the great efforts you make to achieve your common objectives. Under such circumstances, might it actually be odd *not* to truly care about your colleagues? Consider opening yourself, then, to a genuine warmth, caring, and affection for them. Then observe the impact that has on your passion.

Like many leaders, you may have been mostly energizing yourself with ever-higher goals and the demands of yourself and others. Adopting this new, love-based approach may therefore feel as if you are drawing on a very different—and very powerful—energy system. Try energizing yourself in both the new and old ways, and then monitor the results. See which approach, or what combination of the two, works best for you. And ask yourself, "How well have my old ways of energizing myself worked for me? How happy and content have they made me? Am I now as powerful as I want to be?"

Should you decide to show more love and care, you may notice that, initially, they do not flow so easily. If that's the case in either your work life or your personal life, consult the Five Gifts Roadmap. In both domains, the poisons of fear, false shame, and anger will block your love as well as your passion. For example, do you feel you "just don't" have much passion toward your spouse or intimate partner? Instead of accepting that situation as an unchangeable fact, look at the Five Gifts Roadmap. And then look at yourself closely. Likely, you will find fear, anger, or false shame active within you—and at least one of those poisons active within your partner.

If you lack feelings of genuine care, warmth, and affection for your colleagues, conduct the same analysis. Once you identify and transform the poisons blocking your care, it will flow more freely. Then, to make that flow greater, choose to give of yourself more readily. That will generate even more passion within you.

To grow your care even further, focus less on yourself and more on others. Think of your colleagues and imagine what it's like to be them. Imagine what they are feeling. Ask them about themselves and get to know their stories. Consider going further and imagine that each is your brother or sister, or your niece or nephew. Imagine what each was like as a two-year-old child. Imagine, even, the love their parents felt for them as they were born.

This is not some sentimental exercise irrelevant to your business success. This is, rather, an exercise vital for awakening your care and affection, and therefore your passion. This is about you awakening your greater power. Opening yourself to being a more caring leader may not come easy to you. Doing this exercise may feel like quite a challenge. Know, though, that as you practice your capacity to be warm and caring, that capacity—and your power—will expand within you.

An executive once told me, "Dean, once I get to know someone, I can't help but feel affection for them." That will naturally happen for you too—once you identify and resolve the fear, anger, and false shame that would otherwise block you, and once you make the necessary efforts to establish a connection.

By increasing your love in these ways, you will increase your passion. Then draw on that source of energy and put it into action. As you channel your flow of passion into the service of love, it will keep your passion growing.

Remember, then, that the energy that moves within you is your power. But that power, without love, can be dry and sterile. And love without power is weak and ineffectual. But power in the service of love is pure passion.

summary

KEY POINTS TO REMEMBER

- Your passion will flow most powerfully when it's an expression of your love for other people. This principle applies to your personal, intimate life and to your work life as well. In all areas of your life, passion is the same fundamental energy. Naturally, though, how your love and passion manifest will depend on the context.

- At work, your love will be apparent in your care, interest, and concern. It will be apparent in your acts of giving. Showing up in these ways, you will be more passionate and thus more powerful.

- In any area of your life, to enhance the flow of your love and therefore your passion, first identify and transform the poisons that block it, as shown in the Five Gifts Roadmap. Then choose to expand your love further. As a leader, you can do so, for example, by focusing more on others, learning their stories, and empathizing with their feelings.

- As you make these changes and your passion naturally surges, keep putting it in the service of love for other people. This will ensure that your passion continues to soar to higher levels.

ACTIONS TO ENHANCE YOUR POWER

- Identify several people with whom you work closely but toward whom you don't feel very warm and caring. Then identify and transform any of the emotional poisons that are blocking your positive feelings for these colleagues from flowing. Next, take additional steps to build up your feelings of warmth toward them. Imagine what it's like to be them and what they are feeling. Imagine what they were like as very young children. Imagine that each is actually a close family member. Overall, challenge yourself to truly care about these people. And then put your care into action. Do this for at least a week. Then observe the impact this has on your work energy levels.

CALIBRATE THE DEGREE OF YOUR PASSION TO BEST SERVE YOU AND OTHER PEOPLE

In general, as you increase your passion, you increase your power to make things happen and to activate the energies of other people. But be careful to avoid bringing your passion to levels that are not sustainable. Beware, then, of your passion repeatedly rising to great heights and then collapsing, pulling you downward. Or instead of these oscillations, your passion may remain very elevated, but ultimately crash and leave you utterly depleted. To protect yourself from these dangers, balance your passion in the context of other parts of your life and the bigger picture. And bear in mind that even if your passion is manageable for you, it may at times be too much for other people. Modulate it, then, as necessary to continually magnetize their passion to higher levels.

As you unblock your passion and feed it in the ways I'm showing you, the extent of its growth may surprise you. Generally, more passion is a very good thing. It means more power to energize others and to make things happen. But you may find you have more passion than you know what to do with. You may feel so much energy coursing through you that it impairs your ability to be stable and effective.

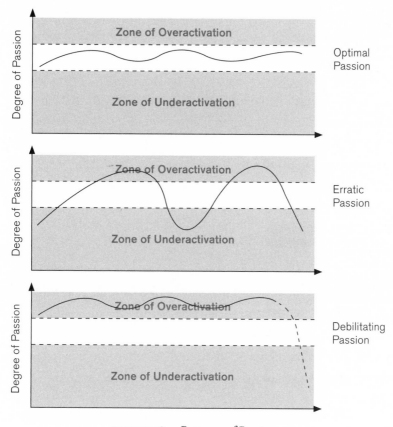

FIGURE 8.1 Patterns of Passion

Should you find yourself in that state, commend yourself for your ability to get there. And be assured that it's easier to lower your passion than to raise it in the first place. Later in this section, I will give you specific guidance for doing so. The overall approach is to continually monitor and calibrate your passion level. You are not powerful when your furnace is too cold—nor when it's too hot, either. Rather, you are most powerful when you are running at just the right temperature.

Naturally, you will experience some fluctuations in your passion. With skillful awareness and practice, you can control them. You can continuously keep your passion in a zone where it is neither underactivated nor overactivated. I call this *optimal passion*. It is shown in the top graph of Figure 8.1. You are more likely to stay in this state if your passion is grounded in your deepest desires and in your love and care for other people.

You will know you are not effectively modulating your passion if one of two things is happening. In one pattern, as shown in the middle graph of Figure 8.1, your passion habitually escalates into zones of over-activation and then slides down rather quickly. You will successively move through periods of great excitement alternating with periods where you feel de-energized and disheartened. This pattern of *erratic passion* can harm you.

> **POWER TALK (to self)**
>
> • "Does my passion tend to fluctuate too wildly?"
>
> • "Am I vulnerable to crashing?"

Do you recognize this pattern within yourself—at least to some degree? If so, being able to so activate yourself is a strength. Now, you just need some fine-tuning. Your fluctuations are occurring because you are allowing your passion and excitement to move to heights that are not quite anchored in reality. So when the inevitable disappointments arise, your passion—and your mood with it—collapse abruptly.

In these circumstances, your passion does not immediately return to a healthy range. Rather, it falls even lower. Then you will find yourself in a zone of underactivation and you will struggle with lethargy and low spirits. This results from a natural law of passion. When you exceed its sustainable bounds, your degree of subsequent depletion will be roughly equal to the extent of your earlier inflation. When that happens, your job is to steadily climb back into the zone of optimal activation and stay there.

One of the problems with erratic passion is that it presents a very confusing picture. A nonprofit executive I assisted would fluctuate between overactivated and underactivated states quite frequently. Sometimes, he would excitedly tell his employees about daring and expansive plans for the future. Naturally, as passion is contagious, they, too, would get excited. But when they would speak with him about these visions later, his energy state was often quite different. He would then dismiss the plans and his employees would feel let down and defeated.

Do you ever act this way? In any part of your life? As this leader discovered, when you behave erratically, people will hesitate to trust you after a while. And that undermines your leadership and your power. Even if you are not obvious in this pattern and are more restrained, the ebb and flow of your passion will still be detected by others. The energy levels and moods of those you lead may move up and down accordingly. Overall, you will be a less stable figure for others to look to.

The second form of unsustainable passion—*debilitating passion*—is shown in the bottom graph of Figure 8.1. If your passion fits this description, you will stay in the zone of overactivation for a lengthy time—for many months or even longer. But ultimately, because it is too taxing for you, your passion will collapse and so will you. One warning sign is an increasing inefficiency.

> **POWER TALK (to self)**
>
> - "Does it feel like my engine is overworking—and yet I'm barely moving?"
> - "Does my passion feel like a grinding tension?"

So ask yourself, "Do I spend great amounts of energy but it feels like I'm barely moving?" "Does my passion feel more like a grinding tension?" "Do I feel like I'm driving on the highway in second gear, struggling to keep up with traffic, my engine overworking?"

If this sounds like you, these are danger signals you must attend to. Ultimately, all this extreme effort cannot be sustained. Then, as shown in Figure 8.1, you will experience a sudden drop-off in your energy. You will have "blown" your engine. Sometimes this is called *burnout*. Sometimes it's just exhaustion. Be very careful, for it may manifest as a serious health problem.

To protect yourself from these two types of unsustainable passion, and to resolve them should they arise, ensure that your passion is balanced in the context of the bigger picture. Ensure that it is balanced with the other aspects of your existence. Is it really true that you absolutely *must* achieve your passion's objective? Perhaps there are other things in your life also very important. And reflect on whether what you're striving for now will be so crucial 10 or 20 years in the future. So try letting go of your goals a bit and backing off from your intensity. See if that actually helps you go faster.

Once you've regained your balance, lean once again into your objectives—but this time with greater flexibility. Let your passion be a slower and steadier burn that assures you of reaching your destination.

Even if your passion is not too much for you, it may be too much for other people. Generally, those around you want to feel your passion and energy because it energizes and sustains them. It naturally feels good for them. Your passion is indeed contagious. However, to magnetize people with your passion, you must emit it to just the right degree. If it's too little, you will not be energizing for others and, in fact, you could be experienced as dull and deadening. But if it's too much, people will not relate to you and your passion will be distancing rather than connecting.

One business vice president brought such intense passion to her work that it propelled her to great heights of achievement. And often, her passion ignited the passion of her subordinates and colleagues. But her passion began to undermine her when the economy went into a downturn, layoffs were announced, and the energy levels on her team started dipping. Rather than modulating her passion to better meet her people where they were, she kept pumping it out at the same high levels of intensity. Then she appeared to others as "out of touch" and even as "over the top." Her extreme energy was no longer uplifting. Rather, it had become irritating. As one of her people told me, "Times are tough and people are losing their jobs. So all the upbeat cheerleading can be annoying."

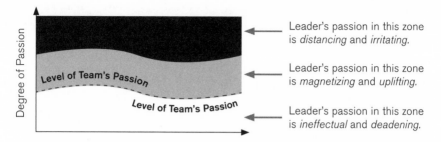

FIGURE 8.2 Leader's Passion in Relation to Team

My client had correctly realized that in order to energize her team, her passion needed to be greater than theirs. But she hadn't realized her passion could move beyond their range and lose its magnetic attraction. She was operating in the top zone of the graph shown in Figure 8.2. And that rendered her ineffective. Consult that graph and ask yourself, "Where is my passion in relation to those I lead? And what effect does that have on them?" Ideally, your passion will continuously hover just above theirs, always pulling their energy upward.

To most effectively use your passion, then, stay continually aware of your energy levels. And stay aware of those levels in other people. Then modulate your passion accordingly. Ensure that it remains in an optimal zone for you, and then synchronize it with the passion of those around you. Calibrate it so that it continuously exerts a powerful, upward pull on their energy. When you harness your passion so precisely and skillfully, it will be an ever more potent engine for you.

KEY POINTS TO REMEMBER

- Increases in your passion generally translate into enhancements of your power. But it's possible for your passion to soar to levels that are not sustainable and that render you unstable. Therefore, it's crucial that you continuously monitor and calibrate your passion.

- One pattern of overactivation is your passion oscillating between excited expansions and countervailing deflations. Or your passion may stay extremely elevated for a longer period, but then crash down into a state of utter depletion. Such severe shifts in your passion will confuse others, impair their willingness to trust you, and undermine your leadership.

- To keep your passion consistent and sustainable, ensure that it is always grounded in your deepest desires and in your genuine love and care for other people. Also, balance your passion with the other parts of your life and with the bigger picture. By slightly relaxing your grip on your goals and desires, you can proceed with more flexibility and with greater power.

- Modulate your passion not just for yourself but also for other people. If it's too elevated, they may experience it as irritating and distancing. But if you maintain it at levels moderately above theirs, they will find it magnetizing and invigorating.

ACTIONS TO ENHANCE YOUR POWER

- Set aside some time and reflect back on the fluctuations in your passion. Can you think of instances when it surged too high and then tumbled down to much lower levels? Have there been periods when it was more of a grinding tension? Or when it was so out of sync with other people that it was actually quite distancing? Write out, in detail, the patterns you identify. Then record your plan for protecting yourself against them. For example, you may decide to consistently monitor your passion levels and get regular feedback from other people. You might also take steps to ensure that your passion remains balanced with the other parts of your life. As you calibrate your passion, you will find it works better for you and for those around you.

9

· THE POWER OF INTELLECT ·
USE THE ELEGANCE OF LOGIC
TO ENHANCE YOUR IMPACT

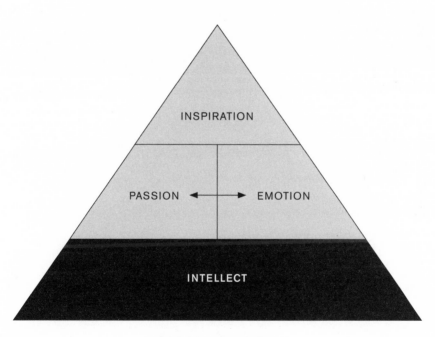

The Four Powers Pyramid

STOP YOUR BELIEFS AND ASSUMPTIONS
FROM ROBBING YOU OF YOUR POWER

One of your greatest challenges is to continuously identify and correct your perceptions, including your beliefs and assumptions. These perceptions drive your emotions which, in turn, trigger actions that can harm you greatly. Therefore, you will be far more powerful when you control these perceptions adeptly. The baseline power of your intellect—your capacity to reason and use logic—enables you to do so. You can use it to assess your beliefs and assumptions and revise them as needed. Otherwise, you risk navigating through your life and your work with a very distorted perspective. You can also use your logical powers to precisely understand how you generate disappointing responses from other people. By tracing back the steps from their responses to your actions and your underlying beliefs and emotions, you will see how you create your own reality. Your beliefs are far more powerful than you realize. Your intellect provides you the capacity for managing them most effectively.

One of the most powerful ways you can use your intellect is to manage your perceptions—your beliefs and assumptions—and those of other people. In this section, we'll cover managing your own perceptions and in the next, we'll discuss how to manage the perceptions of other people. Perceptions are often highly irrational, yet they have a profound impact on much of what you do.

We earlier discussed how your perceptions trigger your emotions and how your emotions, in turn, often determine your actions. These Perception–Emotion–Action (PEA) chains therefore play a central role within you. And sometimes, your perceptions directly mobilize your actions. Yet, although your beliefs and assumptions have such re-percussions, they often lie unexamined outside your awareness. They likely push you into actions that harm you and foreclose you from taking other actions that could benefit you. Almost certainly, they also preclude you from forming relationships with many people.

Adeptly managing your perceptions, then, will make you into a more powerful person and leader. And you need the power at the base of the Four Powers Pyramid—the power of intellect—in order to do so. We already talked about the power of intellect in Chapter 1. Now let's further discuss how this power can aid you.

Remember that your intellect is your capacity to reason and use logic effectively. You can use it to pierce through distorted perceptions and clouds of emotions and see things more clearly. So whenever you are experiencing a negative emotion, whenever you feel a blockage in your passion, and whenever you notice yourself avoiding a human connection, ask yourself, "What beliefs am I holding that are creating this situation?" And then ask, "How do I know my beliefs are true? Can I adopt a different perspective that would make me more powerful?"

You can take your power of intellect even further. You can use it to take apart any disappointing interaction to see exactly how it

> **POWER TALK (to self)**
>
> - "What outcomes am I creating with my beliefs?"
>
> - "How do I know those beliefs are correct?"
>
> - "Are other, more empowering beliefs possible?"

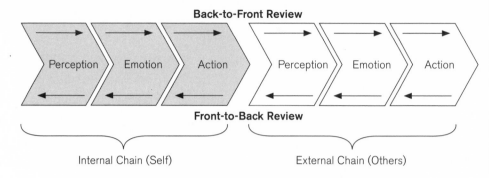

FIGURE 9.1 Analyzing Beliefs (Perceptions) and
Outcomes (Actions) with the Expanded PEA Chain

happened. Then you can use your intellect to map out a change that better serves you. To do so, start with the expanded PEA chain we discussed in Chapter 1. As shown in Figure 9.1, consider both your internal PEA chain and the PEA chain you've triggered in the other person. Then, as shown below, move stepwise front to back or back to front, depending on the information you already have and the information you desire.

Start with the result and trace the steps backward if you wish to understand the causes of an undesirable situation. For example, the founder of a business complained to me that one of his people "took forever to make a crucial decision." He concluded, "Clearly, she's not competent for the role she's in." But I asked him, "How do you know your conclusion is correct?" I invited him to explore the role he may have played in creating the very outcome that now displeased him. So we logically mapped out the sequence of internal and external events that led to it. Then he understood his part more clearly.

Using the PEA chain in Figure 9.1, we started with the external action—actually, the nonaction of the delay—and then worked our way backward. We saw that his employee's fear and feelings of inadequacy had likely caused her inaction. And we surmised that those emotions, in turn, had been triggered by her belief that her abilities were lacking. And that was generated, we determined, by my client's habit of constantly questioning her thinking. That questioning was driven by my client's fear, which in turn was triggered by his deeply held belief that nobody could be counted on to make the right decision.

Consider using this same PEA analysis in regard to the actions of your colleagues, family members, and friends that have displeased you. Bring to bear the power of your intellect intently, yet compassionately. Ask yourself, "What have I created?" Like my client, you may be surprised by what you discover.

If you are unhappy with the behaviors you are activating in other people, use the PEA chain to map out better outcomes for the future. First identify the actions you desire in the other person. Then identify the emotions he must have to prompt them. And then determine the perceptions necessary for triggering those emotions. Continue mapping this out, front to back, step by step. Accordingly, next determine how you must act to create the necessary perceptions. And finally, determine the beliefs and emotions on your part that will lead you to so acting.

When you use your intellect in this way, you take back your power. Rather than being a victim of your circumstances, you are a master of them.

To enhance your power further, predict the probable outcomes of your beliefs. Start with a belief and follow the PEA chain—this time back to front—to determine its likely impact on others and their likely reactions. Using this logical approach, you will see how you create your own reality. You may be startled by what you learn.

For example, let's say your belief about a particular group of coworkers—or residents of your town or city—is, "Those people can't

> **DEEPER WISDOM**
>
> Your beliefs play out and materialize in a myriad of ways, many of them subtle. For example, they will manifest in the manner of your speech, in your vocal tone, in how you dress, and in thousands of other details. Through these manifold signals you emit, people will often detect your beliefs. Then they will respond to you accordingly. Imagine, for example, how people might react to you if you believe, "I am inadequate" or, more provocatively, "You are inadequate." By becoming more conscious of your beliefs, and by better managing them, you will be more effective in eliciting positive responses from other people.

be trusted." Logically and rationally, follow the PEA chain back to front to see how your belief materializes. Determine the emotions your belief will generate in you and the actions that will follow. Then determine how your actions will be perceived, the emotions they will arouse, and the ultimate actions you will have triggered in other people.

Your beliefs are more powerful than you realize. They don't just materialize in your actions. They also materialize in the actions of those around you. To make your beliefs work *for* you rather than *against* you, use the power of your intellect. Specifically, use PEA chains to help you choose the beliefs that will likely generate the most positive outcomes.

Choosing your beliefs in this way does not mean you should disregard your integrity and your values. Nor does it mean you should choose beliefs regardless of their correctness. But before you insist on holding to your current beliefs, bring to bear the full power of your intellect to assess their validity. Consult the evidence pro and con and seek out others' perspectives. If you cannot conclusively prove to yourself that your beliefs are, in fact, correct, then consider changing them. Consider adopting different beliefs if, by doing so, you will create better outcomes for yourself and for other people.

---

summary

KEY POINTS TO REMEMBER

- Your perceptions—which include your beliefs and assumptions—are often irrational. Yet, without your even realizing it, they determine many of your emotions and actions. Therefore, it is essential that you manage your perceptions effectively. Your power of intellect—which is your capacity to reason and use logic—equips you to do so.

- At a minimum, use your intellect to identify and challenge your beliefs and assumptions. But for greater power, also use it to determine how your beliefs and assumptions are generating actions in your colleagues, family members, and friends. The expanded Perception–Emotion–Action (PEA) chain will show you the links of causation between your beliefs, emotions, and actions and the beliefs, emotions, and actions of other people.

- Trace the expanded PEA chain front to back, from the other person's action back to your initial perception, to learn how you are creating your reality. Consider also substituting your desired outcome for the actual outcome and then conduct the same analysis front to back prospectively. Then you will learn what is necessary to create the outcome you most desire.

- Consider adopting different beliefs if your analysis reveals that would create better results for you and for other people. Of course, don't change beliefs that you are certain are correct. And be cautious about changing a belief if doing so would violate your integrity and values. But in all other cases, rely on the power of your intellect to choose the belief that will render you more powerful.

ACTIONS TO ENHANCE YOUR POWER

- Identify three beliefs by which you judge yourself, some other person, or a situation negatively. Then, for each such belief, use the power of your intellect to logically plot out its likely impact on you, on other people, and on your degree of success. Start your analysis at the back end of the PEA chain and then trace your belief's domino effect moving forward. Assess its impact on your emotions and actions and then on the perceptions, emotions, and actions of those around you. Based on what you find, decide whether to adopt different beliefs for the future.

ENHANCE YOUR POWER FURTHER
BY GUIDING PEOPLE'S THINKING AND
REACTIONS TO YOU

People often see you through a distorted lens and then react to you accordingly. Therefore, besides managing your own perceptions, it is essential that you manage those held by other people. A powerful tool that enables you to do so is metacommunication. This means communicating about communication or communicating about the related context. Use metacommunication, for example, to provide a logical framework for your conversation that will focus your listener's attention and help ensure that she correctly understands you. Also consider metacommunicating about your underlying motivations and emotions. People are detecting them nonetheless, although likely in distorted form. Your metacommunication will keep their perceptions more accurate and therefore your conversations more productive. More broadly, metacommunicate not just about yourself, but also about your relationship with the person to whom you are speaking. By doing so, you can continuously guide her

perceptions in a more positive direction and thereby

enhance the quality of your connection.

Just as important as managing your own perceptions is managing the perceptions of other people. Much of what you say and do can be misinterpreted in a variety of ways and, in fact, often will be. And some people will altogether fail to understand you. Each person will then rely on her particular understanding and will respond to you accordingly. This greatly imperils you and your relations with other people.

It is essential, then, that you take steps to protect yourself and others from these dangers. At a minimum, use the power of your intellect to logically structure your communications and to focus people's attention. Then it will be easier for them to understand you. Bear in mind that while you speak, most of your listeners have countless thoughts, feelings, memories, and desires coursing through them. And many of these have nothing to do with what you are saying. To penetrate through that cloud of inattention and focus people's thinking, you must speak so clearly that they can't help but listen and comprehend you.

A powerful tool for structuring your communications and making them most intelligible is metacommunication. This term is used in different ways, and what I mean by it here is communicating about communication or communicating about the context. It's a way of explaining your speech so that people can better absorb it.

> **definition**
>
> **METACOMMUNICATION**
> Communicating about communication or communicating about the related context. Metacommunication structures and guides perceptions and thereby eases the flow of an interaction.

For example, you might say, "I have three points." And then you would enumerate them in sequence. Such an approach almost compels people to listen. They may even interrupt you

If you're in a dynamic meeting competing with other powerful people for "airtime," your declaration of the number of points you have to make "marks out" space for you. Then, when someone interrupts you, you will have more of a basis for pushing back. You will be more empowered to say, for example, "Wait—I still have one more point to make."

to say, "Wait, I'm still on number two. What was that again?" Don't expect people to create a framework for better understanding the information you give them. Instead, do that for them.

Use your intellect to metacommunicate in other ways as well. For example, you can say, "I have two responses to your idea." Or you may say, "I have four objectives for this meeting." Or you might say, "First I'll tell you my decision, and then I'll summarize the rationale. Tell me if you want more detail." When you speak this way, you hold your power. You take command of the interaction. Yet, at the same time, you give others power to more effectively interact with you.

Consider going further and metacommunicating about your underlying motivations and about your emotions too. In this way, you are using the power of your intellect to manage your listener's perceptions of you. Have you noticed that different people respond to you differently? It's largely because of how they see you. As you become more effective in managing their perceptions, you will more likely elicit the responses you desire.

So when you approach a colleague, consider starting with a statement such as, "Here's what I'm hoping to accomplish." Or, "Let me tell

POWER TALK (to others)

- "Let me tell you what I'm hoping we'll accomplish in our talk together."

- "Here's what's going on with me."

you where I am with this." Or even, "Here's what's going on with me." Then briefly provide him the necessary information so that he has a framework for hearing you. Otherwise, he may be thinking, "Why is she bothering me now with this?" Or even, "What's she trying to get out of me?" Or he may have other perceptions and corresponding reactions, many of which you will never know but which could harm you.

Metacommunication is especially helpful in those instances where you are concerned or upset about a matter and wish to discuss it with a colleague. If you simply jump into the conversation fueled by your emotions, he will detect what you are feeling—but likely in exaggerated and distorted form. Then he may have an immediate, negative reaction. Depending on his personality, he may assume, "She's about to blame me." Or, "She's afraid I can't do my job competently." Or, "She's going to try to make me do something." In any of these cases, your colleague will be so preoccupied by his own assumptions and related emotions that he won't be able to truly hear you.

In these situations, you will be more effective by metacommunicating about your emotions. But state them in a diluted form your colleague can comfortably hear. For example, if you are anxious, it's enough to say, "I'm a bit concerned about this and I'm hoping we can work together to find a solution." If, on the other hand, you do not acknowledge your emotions, they will grow larger in your colleague's perceptions of you. Then he will not be at ease and prepared to absorb what you are saying. You will have forfeited much of your power to manage how he perceives you.

Explain not just your statements, but your silence as well. Your silence, in fact, can be a great danger for you. For example, if you are quiet at a meeting, people may misinterpret that in any one of a variety of negative ways. Some may construe your silence as arrogance. Others will think you are angry with them. Yet others will assume you lack self-confidence. People may even conclude that you have nothing of importance to say and therefore lack expertise and intelligence.

To guard against such misinterpretations, use metacommunication to acknowledge your silence and to help people understand it. For example, you might say, "I realize I'm not saying much now, but I'm listening and I'll give you my reactions later."

To further manage the perceptions held by your colleagues and others, metacommunicate about your interactions and relationships with them. For example, when you refer to "our relationship" while speaking with a coworker, you are metacommunicating that you do, indeed, have a connection. And you are telegraphing that it's important to you. As a result, your colleague's perception of you—and of the connection between the two of you—will grow more positive.

More directly, you might say, "Our relationship is important to me." Or you might speak to what is unique and valuable about your connection. You might even comment on the noticeably difficult aspects of your interactions, but place them in the context of an overall positive picture. You may say, for example, "I know we have our disagreements and that enables us to find such creative solutions." Or, "I know we think quite differently and that makes our conversations stimulating." When you metacommunicate in these ways, you steer the other person's perceptions of your interactions—and of your relationship—into a more positive direction.

Consider also metacommunicating in the immediate moment of a challenging interaction. Then you can lift the conversation to a higher level. Say, for example, "This is what I think is happening between us." Then offer a nonblaming and affirming explanation. I heard one executive simply say, "I see we have passionately different views on this subject. And I trust we'll come to a resolution."

> **POWER TALK (to others)**
>
> - "Our relationship is important to me."
> - "Let me tell you what I find so valuable about our interactions."
> - "This is what I think is happening between us."

Even better, use metacommunication before the conversation gets difficult. So when you notice your views conflict with those of your colleague, present them in a way that does not activate his instant opposition. Accordingly, before stating your views, ask for permission. Ask, "Are you open to hearing a different opinion?" Or say, "I have a view on this that is likely different from yours. Do you want to know what it is?" By so asking, you are communicating your intent to be respectful. You are helping your colleague feel less threatened—and more prepared for your comments. You are thereby creating an opening for dialogue.

When you ask permission in this manner, people will not typically say no. But some may avoid saying yes. And that signifies their unwillingness to hear other viewpoints. In such a case, your request has revealed that should you speak your opinion, you will only trigger your colleague's opposition—and that the ensuing conversation will therefore likely be unproductive.

If, on the other hand, your colleague signals a willingness to hear your views, state them in a tone and manner that is less apt to activate his false shame and anger. Then ask for his reaction. Say, for example, "Tell me your response to what I'm saying. I'm interested to hear your perspective." By so speaking, you are communicating your respect and mitigating the threat people will often feel when you disagree with them. And once your colleague responds and tells you his perceptions, you will be all the more equipped to effectively adjust them.

Using the power of your intellect in these ways to manage people's perceptions, you create greater understanding. You help prevent the fear, false shame, and anger that so easily get activated in interpersonal communication. You therefore protect yourself and others from the destructive impact of these negative emotions.

summary

KEY POINTS TO REMEMBER

- As people will often hold distorted views of you and then act on them in ways that can harm you, it is crucial that you use the power of your intellect to manage those perceptions effectively.

- Metacommunication is a powerful tool for guiding and adjusting people's perceptions of you. It means communicating about communication or communicating about the related context.

- One form of metacommunication is providing a logical framework as you speak so that you focus people's attention and ensure that they accurately understand you. For example, consider enumerating your points as you make them to help people better track you.

- More powerfully, consider metacommunicating about your underlying motivations and emotions. People will often detect them regardless. Absent your acknowledgment of them, they may perceive them in a distorted form and react accordingly.

- Metacommunicate not just about yourself, but also about your interactions and relationship with the person to whom you are speaking. Affirm your connection, assert its value, and place its challenging aspects in the context of an overall positive picture.

- Consider also metacommunicating in the event your views oppose those of the person with whom you are conversing. First ask permission to express your views, and then after you have done so, ask for the listener's thoughts and reactions. By so acting, you help others feel less threatened and, as a result, you can have more productive interactions.

ACTIONS TO ENHANCE YOUR POWER

- For the next week, whenever you make a suggestion or provide an explanation of any complexity, experiment with metacommunication by enumerating your points. This will work best if you enumerate at least three points, but not more than four. Start off by saying words to the effect of, "I have three (or four) points. First . . ." Then enumerate each successive point as you make it. See if this helps organize and focus your own thinking as well as the thinking of other people.

- After you have completed the above exercise, take your metacommunication practice one step further. Experiment for another week, commenting on what is transpiring in your conversations as you have them. You might comment on your motivations, your emotions, and/or the interaction in general. In doing so, even if you acknowledge some negativity, try to keep the overall tone of your comments positive. Aim to create a supportive framework for the interaction. Then notice the impact this approach has on your conversations—and on your power.

USE ADVANCED PSYCHOLOGICAL INSIGHT
FOR ASTUTELY UNDERSTANDING OTHER PEOPLE

People will sometimes develop very distorted perceptions of you due to one of several common mechanisms. Then they will respond to you accordingly. Often, those responses will be negative and will confuse and disturb you. These patterns of distorted perception are transference, displacement, and projection. Using transference, people will see you as if you were someone else. With projection, they will mistakenly think you have the same emotion or tendency that they do. And with displacement, they will direct toward you the same negative emotions they are actually feeling toward another person. As you learn about these mechanisms, you will better recognize them while they're in operation. Then you can hold your power in the face of them rather than reflexively and emotionally reacting. And most important, your knowledge of these patterns protects you from inadvertently using them. It protects you, therefore, from the great harm they can cause you and your relations with other people.

People misperceive reality in a variety of ways, frequently by using one of three common mechanisms. By learning about them, you will recognize when people are succumbing to them and distorting how they see you. Then you will better understand their conduct that previously seemed puzzling and even "crazy" to you.

It is the power of your intellect that will fuel this greater understanding. As you draw on that intelligence as needed in your interactions, you will less likely react to others in ways that do not serve you. Instead, you will find yourself silently noting in regard to the other person, "Oh, I know about this pattern." Psychologists learn about these mechanisms of distortion as part of their doctoral training. But you can learn and use this wisdom, too. It will render you more effective—and more powerful—in your conversations.

As you read about these psychological mechanisms, try to remember when you've seen them operating in other people. Then you will more readily recognize them when they arise in future interactions. And that will equip you to more effectively deal with them. Even better, ask yourself, "When have I ever used these patterns?" If you are like most people, you have done so from time to time. Your self-recognition will help you avoid falling into them.

TRANSFERENCE

One pattern of distorted perception is *transference.* According to its most useful definition, it means seeing another person, and responding to him, *as if* he were someone else. If a coworker or stranger has an odd and inappropriate reaction to you, suspect that she has slipped into this state of faulty perception. Instead of seeing you for who you really are, she is actually, in a deeper sense, seeing another person.

So if you are a man, a colleague may think of you, "He reminds me of my competitive

> **definition**
>
> **TRANSFERENCE**
> Your colleague seeing you, and responding to you, *as if* you were someone else. Typically, your colleague's transference toward you will be based on a person from her early family history.

brother." And then he will act toward you as if you were actually his brother. He will neglect to appreciate that you are an entirely separate person. And if you are a woman, he may see you, and respond to you, as if you were his intrusive sister or helpless aunt or demanding mother.

Transference is usually gender-specific. And usually, it is based on early family relationships. So if you are a woman, you will more likely trigger a transference of people's sisters, mothers, and other women who have long been significant for them. If you are a man, you will tend to activate brother, father, and other male transferences. And the more similar you are to someone from your colleague's past, the more likely you will activate his transference in regard to that person.

So if you are a woman and significantly older than your direct report, he may tend to see you as his mother. Then he might think to himself, "She's kind of distant and controlling, just like Mom"—even though that's not really an accurate description of you. And then you will notice him responding to you rather strangely. He may try too hard to please you. Or to oppose you. Either way, he's not seeing the reality of who you truly are and responding most appropriately. And that limits the effectiveness of your interactions with each other.

Typically, people are not aware when they are falling into this kind of flawed thinking. And typically, they are not aware that they are trying to pull you in there with them. They want you to enact the role they've assigned you. So if a coworker—or your intimate partner—has a father transference to you, she may activate in you her father's typical behavior. For example, if he was critical, you may sud-

DEEPER WISDOM

Not all transference assumes negative characteristics in other people. Sometimes, the transference is "positive," in which case its target is viewed as having beneficial qualities. For example, you could be experienced as the indulgent mother, the all-protective father, or the kindly grandfather. Ultimately, though, these transferences are still harmful as they are based on distorted pictures of reality. Generally, when you're their target, you will not be able to live up to them. When people discover that, they will be quite disappointed in you and may grow distant and even angry with you.

denly find yourself being critical with her, too. Then you will have confirmed for her a noxious picture of reality. In this case, it may be, "Men see me as incompetent." She may then think to herself, or even tell you, "See, I told you!"

The problem gets even larger. Have you noticed how some work teams seem more like dysfunctional families? The team members are perhaps squabbling like jealous siblings. And the leader may be enacting the role of "all-powerful father" or "hard-to-please mother"—or perhaps the mother who has her favorite child. These dynamics arise from transference that is not recognized and controlled. The team members are seeing each other as if they are particular parents, sisters, and brothers. And then they are actually accepting the familial roles they are assigning each other. Teams are fertile grounds for this because their structures remind people of their early family lives.

POWER TALK (to self)
• "Am I seeing my colleagues, spouse, and children for who they really are?"   • "Or am I instead seeing other people?"

So try to resist your colleagues' transference pull. Instead, be true to your normal and healthier ways of acting. And be careful lest you inadvertently drift into a state of transference, too. After all, it is quite common. And it will render you less effective, and less powerful, in your interactions. So ask yourself, "Am I seeing my colleagues for who they *really* are? And in my own family, am I *truly* seeing my spouse and children? Or am I seeing other people instead?"

DISPLACEMENT

Displacement is another psychological mechanism that distorts people's perceptions. But here, emotions play a more central function. When your coworkers use displacement, they let the emotions they actually feel toward someone else color how they see you. They "displace" those emotions onto you.

definition
DISPLACEMENT   Your colleague directing toward you the same emotions he actually feels toward another person.

For example, your colleague is angry with his wife and now, without apparent reason, is testy with you. He is displacing his anger onto you. Often, anger is displaced when it cannot be safely directed at its original target. So if your boss feels beaten down by *his* boss, he may direct his resultant anger at you. Or he'll go home that day and perhaps berate his children. When people refer to "taking it out on" someone else, they are talking about displacement.

Although anger is the emotion most often displaced, other emotions can be displaced, too. For example, people may displace their fear of someone else—or something else—onto you. Then they will be very afraid of you. Or they may displace their fear onto the group of which you are a member. Then they may start acting toward you and your group in a fearful and even aggressive manner. Unless you recognize the displacement mechanism in operation, it may all be puzzling, and quite troubling, for you. This mechanism can create ethnic prejudice and even hatred. Yet, it arises in milder form within organizations, too.

When you feel a colleague's displaced emotions coming at you, be careful to not let them penetrate you. Be careful, in other words, that you not react reflexively and emotionally. Instead, check to ensure that your own actions are not the cause of his strong emotions. If you determine they clearly aren't, calmly tell yourself, "Oh, my colleague seems to be displacing. It has nothing to do with me." And then take care to ensure that you do not err similarly. Take care to ensure that you do not cause harm by displacing your own emotions.

PROJECTION

The third and final pattern of distortion you should know about is *projection*. It arises when a colleague assumes something about you when, in fact, it is only a truth about him. He is "projecting" his own feelings or propensities onto you. When people use this mechanism, they are completely unaware that they are doing so. And they are unaware of the damage they are causing to themselves and to their relations with other people.

For example, a coworker angry with you may assume that you are also angry with her. She is projecting her anger onto you. Or a colleague who is very critical and judgmental toward herself may assume that you also have critical and judgmental thoughts about her. Then she may feel shamed and even oppressed by you. Unless you understand what is happening, her conduct around you may confuse and perplex you.

If you look closely, you will also often see projection in cases of intense competition. A highly competitive colleague may see you as very competitive, too, and therefore feel very threatened by you—even though you are not competitive at all. Such a colleague is projecting his competitive nature onto you. And then he may frighten himself with the illusion he has created and feel in danger because of you.

Projection explains how many conflicts arise, including on a global scale. Angry and combative leaders often assume that others have their same tendencies. And so, in a misguided effort to protect themselves, they may strike "preemptively."

Transference, displacement, and projection may seem somewhat extreme to you. Yet they are all quite common. Therefore, it is essential that you be prepared to effectively respond to them. In all cases, do not let yourself get provoked and do not become emotionally reactive. Do not, in other words, give away your power. Instead, use the power of your intellect to detect exactly what is happening. And importantly, be alert and on guard as you move forward so that you yourself don't slip into any of these disempowering states of distortion.

summary

KEY POINTS TO REMEMBER

- People often use one of several mechanisms that significantly distort how they see you and accordingly respond to you. By learning about these patterns, you can detect when people are falling into them. Then their puzzling and disheartening conduct will make more sense to you.

- One such mechanism is transference. It arises when your colleague sees you, and responds to you, as if you were another person—typically a person from his early family history. The more similar you are to that third person, the more likely you will trigger in your colleague this distorted perception.

- Another distorting mechanism is displacement. When this is operating, your colleague is directing toward you the same emotions he actually feels toward another person. Anger is the emotion most commonly displaced. This explains the phenomenon of people taking their anger "out on" some other person.

- Projection is yet another mechanism of distortion. In this case, people assume that you feel the same as they feel or have the same tendencies that they do. They "project" those aspects of their personalities onto you. And as with transference and displacement, they are not aware they are doing so.

- Endeavor to recognize these patterns when they are determining how people see you and respond to you. Then you will be more powerful. Rather than reacting emotionally and feeding the negative tone of the interaction, you will be more able to stay calm and unruffled.

- Your knowing about these patterns also helps protect you from using them yourself. And that protects your relationships and also your power.

ACTIONS TO ENHANCE YOUR POWER

- Think of several recent interactions where a colleague (or family member or friend) showed negative feelings toward you that seemed unrelated to your past or present conduct. Examine each interaction carefully. Determine if it might have been partly driven by your colleague's transference, displacement, or projection. If, upon your close scrutiny, you have the clear sense that your colleague's reaction had "nothing to do with" you, this is helpful evidence. It may well indicate that one of the distorting mechanisms was indeed present. Use this information to heighten your sensitivity. Then, the next time you have a similar interaction, you may more readily recognize one of the distorting mechanisms while it's operating.

10

· THE POWER OF INSPIRATION ·
SPEAK TO PEOPLE'S DEEPEST NEEDS AND ACTIVATE YOUR GREATEST POWER

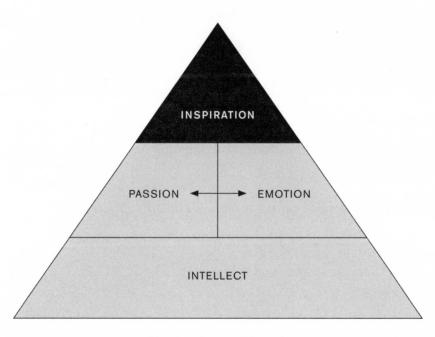

The Four Powers Pyramid

PREPARE TO ENTER THE REALM OF
INSPIRED LIVING AND LEADING

*Ready yourself for activating your power of inspira-
tion. This power is the capacity to "bring spirit in." Spirit
is the force of unity between people. It will take you
beyond your separate self and provide you the sense of
belonging to a larger whole and a greater collective.
People naturally hunger for that experience. When
you provide it to yourself, and to others, you will be
deeply moved and will deeply move them. As you will
see, inspiration is the greatest power. Using it, though,
requires mastering your negative emotions rather
than reacting to them. With such mastery, people
will be more willing to trust you and to let themselves
be inspired by you. And your self-mastery will keep
your inspiration potent, pure, and uncontaminated.*

Now is the time for us to consider the greatest power of all—the
power of inspiration. You have studied the other three powers and now
have many tools for developing them. Your practice and increasing
mastery of these powers prepares you for entering the domain of true
inspiration.

Recall that the power of inspiration is the capacity to be *in spirit* and
to bring *spirit in*. Spirit is the unifying force among people. It is larger

than our separate selves and it connects us all with each other. People naturally hunger to move beyond their isolated self-enclosures and to be part of something greater. They want to find a larger identity in their team, their community, some other group, or their nation. When you provide them the opportunity for such self-expansion, you deepen your power as a person and as a leader.

You can choose to be a truly inspirational individual. You can choose to use this power—or, really, to let it use you. As you will find, it will not actually be *your* power. Rather, it will be a power of which you are a guardian and a servant. And that's because this power is necessarily greater than any one person.

Mastering the power of inspiration is a significant undertaking. Teaching you about it actually requires a separate book. However, in this chapter, I will provide you some essential information. You will have enough to start accessing this capacity and then begin to witness it burgeon within you.

But beware that as inspiration is such an extraordinary power, many people will not be open to your use of it unless they fully trust you. Therefore, you must first develop your power of emotion sufficiently. People must see that you do not get overcome by negative feelings and then act on them. They must see that your fears, resentments, and self-doubt do not take hold of you and determine your actions.

To appreciate this more deeply, consider the hopes and longings that your inspiration can activate in other people. Consider how much they really do want to be part of a greater community and a greater endeavor. And consider how likely it is that they've already heard inspirational leaders and have

> **DEEPER WISDOM**
>
> Some leaders who use the power of inspiration can get quite inflated by the attention and influence it magnetizes to them. This is a significant danger for them. It often results in their becoming less self-vigilant and more prone to acting on their underlying insecurities and resentments. That can lead to disappointments in followers and sometimes to scandals. Your continuous self-awareness is therefore crucial when accessing your power of inspiration.

ultimately been disappointed. Therefore, to protect themselves, many will initially respond to your inspiration guardedly and even cynically. Unless they completely trust you, they will not give themselves over to your inspired visions. They will not allow themselves to be so vulnerable with you.

A CEO who built a start-up into a thriving enterprise often invoked the power of inspiration—at first, quite successfully. He was admired by his people and could magnetize all the support he needed. But he was also irritable at times, and during a difficult period, that began to leak out in disparaging remarks about his executives and managers. Many in the organization felt betrayed and offended. When he then attempted to be inspirational at large company gatherings, he was met with audible hissing and sneering. His authority was broken, and not surprisingly, the company did not exist as a separate entity much longer.

This CEO hadn't realized that in seeking to be inspirational, he would be held to a higher standard. You can probably think of other inspirational leaders who have fallen because their power of emotion was not sufficiently developed.

It is essential that you master your emotions for the additional reason that they can otherwise contaminate your inspired words and actions. Inspiration so tainted can become toxic and cause significant harm. Consider, for example, the inspirational leader who angrily judges and condemns those outside his circle. He is creating a mentality of "us versus them." This only generates more anger in return—and more walls between people. This is not true inspiration.

Taking this one step further, a group of people or even an entire nation can be "inspired" to attack others and cause great destruction. They have found for themselves a larger identity in their association. And they are energized by visions of the victories they can achieve together. In these cases, however, fear, anger, and false shame have fused with and corrupted their power of inspiration. People have no desire to battle others when these emotions are not present.

So before you seek to inspire others, take an inventory of your nega-

tive emotions. Ask yourself, "How is fear, anger, or false shame contaminating my actions?
How might they impair my inspirational leadership?" Once you have identified these dangers, use the instructions from the previous
chapters for containing them. Your awareness
of your negative emotions—and your guarding against them—is especially crucial as you
contemplate being an inspirational leader.

Such leadership does not require you to be free of negative feelings.
However, it does require you to be aware of them as they arise within
you. It also requires you to make sincere efforts to guard against them.
And should you, in fact, act on these emotions, it is essential that you
acknowledge your error promptly. Your so acting can undo much of the
harm. Actually, your error may make you seem more human to others.
Then they will more likely identify with you and join with you in your
inspired efforts.

So as you read the following sections and prepare to enter the realm
of inspirational leadership, be acutely aware that to inspire others, you
must be trusted. And gaining that trust requires you to master your
emotions. Your reward for all your hard work will be access to the greatest power—because the people who grant it to you will trust you to
use it for a greater purpose, for the good of all, not for your own self-
interested objectives.

KEY POINTS TO REMEMBER

- The greatest power is the power of inspiration. This is the capacity to be "in spirit" and to "bring spirit in." Spirit is the unifying force among people. It takes us beyond our limited and separate selves and provides us an experience of being one with a greater collective. People naturally hunger for this larger identity. You can provide it to them, and to yourself as well, by being a truly inspirational leader.

- Operating in the realm of inspirational leadership requires that you master your negative emotions rather than acting on them. Absent such mastery, others will not trust you and will not allow themselves to be inspired by you.

- Failing to master your fear, anger, and false shame could also result in these poisons contaminating your inspiration. And that could cause you and others significant harm. Effectively managing your emotions is therefore essential for keeping your inspiration strong, clean, and appropriately directed.

ACTIONS TO ENHANCE YOUR POWER

- Set aside some time to review your current degree of mastery over your fear, anger, and false shame. To what extent are they influencing your actions? To what extent, then, do you sense people may be noticing? You can still be an inspirational leader if you have these feelings. In fact, they are natural and to be expected. But it is important that they not be a driving force behind your otherwise inspired actions. Therefore, to keep your emotions in check, gather together a group of your close friends and supporters. Ask them to immediately advise you whenever they detect negative emotions in your conduct, particularly in conduct that aims to be inspirational. By means of their support, your inspiration will less likely be contaminated, and your use of this power, therefore, is more likely to be effective.

UNITE WITH OTHER PEOPLE AND CONTINUALLY SHOW YOUR COMMITMENT TO THEM

Using the power of inspiration is not about your ego growing larger. Rather, it is about your ego getting smaller. It is about giving yourself over to something bigger than your separate self. It is, in fact, about giving yourself over to a greater collective. So to use this power, you must unite with others and show you truly are committed to them and to your mutual endeavor. You must show that you really will "be there" for them. Accordingly, ensure that your team members feel they are included by you and are an essential part of your overall efforts. And ensure that in your role as leader, you always put the group first before your own self-interest. When you are so committed to the group and its members, they will be delighted to serve you. Your leadership will then be less of a struggle and will flow with more ease and power.

Choosing to operate in the realm of inspiration is a major decision. It requires you to transcend the usual boundaries of self-interest and dedicate yourself to serving other people. It requires you to join in a union with them. This is a significant sacrifice. Yet great satisfaction, fulfillment, and meaning can come with it. And giving yourself over to others will inspire them to give in return.

So let's identify what, exactly, you can do to show your unity with others and your commitment to them. If you follow these steps faithfully and with sincerity, you may be astonished by the force of the responses you engender. But this type of effect is only natural. Remember that in being an inspirational leader for others, you are speaking to some of their deepest longings and desires.

To start, acknowledge that each effort made by you and by your team is a collective one. But it is not enough to simply say that. Demonstrate by your words and actions that you really *mean* it. So continuously use the word *we* and eschew the word *I* when speaking of accomplishments. Speak of each one as if it had been achieved by the entire group in concert. Let the tone of your comments and your leadership be, "We're all in this together."

How inspired would you be by a leader who only marginally included you in his efforts? And who did not communicate your importance to him? Ensure, then, that all the members of your team know they are an integral part of your mutual venture. Let them know that you indeed need them. And show that not just by your statements, but also by your questions. Ask them, for example, "What's your opinion?" Or ask, "What do you want your contribution to be?" By so showing your interest and engaging them, you show how much you value them. You are conveying how vital they are to your joint endeavor.

> **POWER TALK (to others)**
>
> - "We need you."
> - "What do you want your contribution to be?"

While you offer others opportunities to be more involved and committed, show your own commitment as well. And demonstrate that your commitment is not just to the group, but is also to each individual member. Show your people that, as much as you can, you will be there for them. This will expand their trust in you. And then they will be more willing to truly join in with you.

More generally, consistently put the group first, before your own self-interest. People will observe you closely and will be very sensitive to how you use your power. If they believe you use it *for* them, for the greater good, then they will trust and accept your leadership. But if they believe that you use your power more for yourself, they will feel used and betrayed and therefore resist you. Or they will not even trust you to begin with. So continuously ask yourself, "What is best for my team— and for my overall organization?" And then act accordingly. In this way, you ensure that your inspirational leadership will survive and flourish.

Meanwhile, also share your passion with those you lead. Remember that your passion is contagious and it will draw them in. And it will even more energize the sense of spirit you've been building. Your co-workers will want to *feel* your passion. They'll want to be a part of the collective excitement you are creating.

However, you don't need to beat your chest, gesture animatedly, and speak in loud tones in order to activate the power of inspiration. In fact, you can be introverted and your passion may be a bit understated. One executive I know is quite inspirational, even though he is also very mild-mannered. His team is so convinced of his loyalty and feels so indebted to him that, as one of them told me, "We'd walk off a cliff for him."

Can you imagine what you could make happen with such energized support from others? Can you imagine the efforts you could constellate? And how barriers would fall down before you? This degree of power is available to you. It's available in the techniques that, in this chapter, I'm providing you. You can use them to great effect if you practice them selflessly, with diligence and self-discipline.

When your team's efforts are driven by the power of inspiration, many aspects of your

> **DEEPER WISDOM**
>
> When you are an inspirational leader, people will want to be in the presence of your power and bask in your "glow." And when you show a genuine interest in them, it will be very validating and moving for them. Then they will be all the more inspired to join with you and make their contribution. Be mindful of these special powers you have as an inspirational leader. By using them wisely, you can be an ever more magnetic force for others.

leadership will require less force and struggle. Your team members will likely *want* to perform their tasks and will less likely need reminders, or prodding, from you. When you make your requests and issue your directives, they will flow forth with greater ease and will be received with greater ease, too. That's because they'll come not so much from you as a self-interested person, but from you in your role as the team guardian and champion.

Even if you sometimes need to more forcefully assert your authority, your power of inspiration will still render you more effective. For example, if a team member has not delivered on a commitment, you will more likely respond selflessly rather than feel slighted and react angrily. Your response might simply be, "As the leader of our team, I must hold you to your commitment." Or you might say, "If I let this slide, I'd be betraying our team and our vision." Speaking so cleanly on behalf of the greater good, you will be a more impactful and more powerful leader.

So consider what type of leader you intend to be. Consider whether you are willing to make the effort and sacrifices that the power of inspiration requires. And consider the benefits, too. Reflect on how much you might accomplish if you were more united with others as you pursued your collective and inspired vision.

KEY POINTS TO REMEMBER

- Using the power of inspiration requires that you move beyond self-focused objectives and give yourself over to something greater. It requires that you join with others and show your genuine commitment to them.

- Accordingly, to be an inspirational leader, help people feel included and an integral part of your joint endeavor. For example, when you speak of accomplishments, continuously use the word *we* and shun the word *I.* Let others know that you achieved your goals together.

- Further, take extra care to ensure that each of your actions as a leader best serves the team rather than your own self-interest. When people see that you use your power for them and for the greater good, they will trust and embrace your inspirational leadership.

- Overall, when others observe your commitment to the group and feel the inspiration behind your efforts, they will want to join in and make their contributions. Your leadership will then require less force and struggle. And your power will flow with greater ease and impact.

ACTIONS TO ENHANCE YOUR POWER

- To accept you as an inspirational leader, people need to see that you act for the greater good rather than out of self-interest. Therefore, take some time to reflect on your leadership. Have you been taking any actions as a leader that are mostly about promoting yourself? Or protecting yourself? Pay careful attention to what you discover. Then take the necessary corrective actions.

DEEPLY HONOR EACH PERSON'S
CONTRIBUTIONS TO YOUR MUTUAL ENDEAVOR

To inspire those around you, honor them by expressing your sincere appreciation. At a minimum, recognize the specific actions they've performed and the value of those actions to you, your team, and the larger organization. Then speak your heartfelt gratitude authentically and sincerely. You begin to satisfy people's deeper needs and longings when you validate them so generously. Yet you can create an even greater impact by acknowledging to your colleagues the strengths their conduct reveals. Then go even further by showing the ongoing benefit of those strengths to the team and the larger collective. When you recognize people so deeply, they will be magnetized to you. And then they will be inspired to make their greatest contribution.

We have talked about uniting with others such that they feel they're an integral part of your mutual venture. Now take that one step further. Validate them so deeply for their talents and their contributions that they feel truly honored by you. Let them see that their value is essential for you and your joint efforts. Then the inspiration they feel will be all the greater.

Inspirational leadership necessarily focuses on the team or the larger group. Counterbalance that focus with your attention on the individual

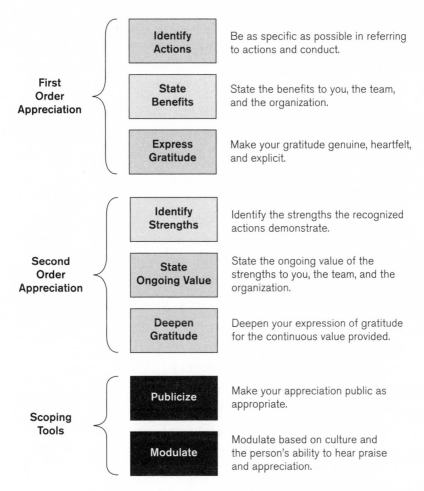

FIGURE 10.1 First and Second Order Appreciation

members. Each human being has a fundamental need to be appreciated and valued. And each person also has an innate and powerful need for belonging. When you meet these needs for others, they will draw in closer to you. And they will be moved to contribute most generously.

To most effectively recognize others and provide them a sense of belonging, use the tools that I call *first and second order appreciation*. They are shown in Figure 10.1. If you only provide your employees first order appreciation, that will have a powerful impact on them. And if you go further and provide second order appreciation, the impact will be much larger. Bear in mind, also, that you can use these approaches with your family and friends. All people need and desire this degree of validation. It is emotional—and inspirational—fuel for them.

Let's start with first order appreciation. As shown in Figure 10.1, it consists of three steps. First, state your colleague's actions that you wish to recognize. And be very specific in doing so. For example, when you simply say, "Nice job" or "You're doing great," your compliments are so vague that they're not very meaningful. When you provide more details, you help your coworker understand what, exactly, she did that was so helpful. And, importantly, you demonstrate you have thought carefully about her actions and are therefore sincere in your comments.

Once you have identified your colleague's actions, explain how they have benefited you, your team, and the greater organization. With clarity and precision, state all the results of her contributions. And don't just attend to concrete events. Keeping in mind the external Perception–Emotion–Action (PEA) chains we discussed in the prior chapter, state the favorable perceptions and positive emotions she generated as well. Let her know the full range of her impact.

And then, as the final step, express your heartfelt gratitude and appreciation. It is easy to simply say, "Thanks," but try making a deeper emotional investment. Consider saying, for example, "I am sincerely grateful for all your efforts." Or, "What you did really means a lot to me." But don't just say these things. *Feel* them as well. When you invest so much care and feeling in your words, and in your colleague, then he will more fully join with you in your inspired endeavors.

> **POWER TALK (to others)**
>
> - "I sincerely appreciate all your efforts."
> - "All your hard work really means a lot to me."
> - "I'm so glad you're on our team."

Imagine, for a moment, what it would be like for you to receive such acknowledgment for your efforts. Imagine, if it came from your boss or your colleagues, what loyalty and service it might mobilize within you. And then imagine the impact that you, likewise, can have on others.

One hospital administrator continually collected the recognitions he received that were most meaningful for him. He was very powerful but still felt a need for this validation. He kept it all in a separate folder that he'd quietly consult from time to time to lift him up when he was feeling down and depleted. These recognitions were like prized trophies for him. One day as we sat together at his desk, he opened a drawer, removed the folder, and showed me one of his favorites. It simply said, "What you're doing for us is valuable beyond words. I am so thankful we have you with us." You, too, can provide others such trophies that will move them. The effort on your part will be so little compared with the impact you are creating.

Yet, as powerful as all this is, you can take it one step further. You can create an even greater effect at the level of second order appreciation. Here, you do not simply recognize others' actions. You go beyond that and recognize the *strengths* their actions demonstrate. Therefore, rather than merely validating someone's conduct, you are validating him or her as a person.

For instance, one of your direct reports has performed exceptionally in advancing an initiative. She has collaborated skillfully with colleagues and adroitly defused budding conflict. At the level of first order appreciation, you would only recognize these actions. But by using the second order approach, you will also acknowledge the strengths these actions reveal. You might recognize, for example, your employee's sensitivity and finesse, her warm and engaging manner, and her boldness in addressing difficult interactions.

Such recognition is powerful because it affirms your employee's value as a person. And the more specific you are, the more honored and "seen" she will feel. In fact, try to find the strengths that are unique to each person—and then reflect those back to him. People yearn to have their special qualities recognized and confirmed. When you do that for them, they will be more responsive to the pull of your inspiration.

Sometimes I am asked, "But wouldn't providing so much praise and recognition just inflate people's egos and make them more self-centered?"

Actually, the opposite is typically true. When you meet people's needs to be esteemed and valued, they can release much of their self-preoccupation. And then they will be more able to give themselves over to the team and its mutual endeavor.

So once you have acknowledged your colleague's strengths, take it yet one step further. Describe how those strengths provide an ongoing benefit to the team. Unlike momentary actions that tend to yield benefits limited in time, strengths are continuously operating and therefore continually provide value to the team and the larger organization. So you might say, for example, "Because you are so warm and astute with people, our team gets excellent support from others." Or you might say, "Your passion makes our team members excited to work together."

After you have recognized your direct report's strengths and the ongoing benefits they provide, express your sincere gratitude to him. In doing so, be no less warm and earnest than I described for first order appreciation. But now, let your gratitude go deeper. That's because the benefit you are acknowledging is so much deeper, too. So you might say, for example, "I am very grateful for your commitment to us." Or, "I'm so glad you're on our team."

You can further heighten the impact of your recognition by expressing it in a public forum. Then your employee will likely feel even more honored by you. However, be thoughtful before so acting. Your public statements may activate in others feelings of envy and competition. Depending on the situation, it may be best to act more discreetly.

And sometimes, due to your employee's culture or personality, she may feel uncom-

---

DEEPER WISDOM

Have you ever noticed that your compliments sometimes don't "get through"? That's because your words of appreciation can activate in the recipient an inner voice of false shame. And that voice will counter your message. For example, you may recognize your colleague's analytical abilities and insight, and the negating voice of false shame will silently reply, "I'm not that smart." Sometimes, in fact, the voice of false shame is so strong that much of the validation you provide will be immediately discarded as untrue. In cases where you suspect that may happen, make your recognition sufficiently mild that it is less likely to trigger the false shame to begin with.

fortable being recognized so publicly. Depending on what you say, she may even feel uncomfortable when you provide your recognition privately. Therefore, be sensitive to your employee and to the cues that she provides you. Then calibrate your appreciation accordingly. Your employee wants your recognition—and she wants it to not exceed what she can comfortably take in.

Overall, each person hungers deeply for affirmation of his or her value. And each hungers deeply for belonging. Consider, then, feeding those hungers with your heartfelt recognition. That will inspire your people to give more freely and to integrate into your group more fully. And that makes you a more powerful and more inspirational leader.

summary

KEY POINTS TO REMEMBER

- To deepen your power of inspiration, inspire others with your words of recognition and appreciation. When people feel so honored by you, they will draw in closer to you and contribute most greatly.

- Recognize your colleagues and team members by taking at least three steps. First, acknowledge the specifics of their actions. Second, show how those actions benefited you and your collective efforts. And third, express your sincere and heartfelt gratitude.

- To make your recognition even more memorable and inspirational, acknowledge the strengths your colleague's actions reveal. In so speaking, you are going beyond validating her actions to validating her as a person. Then go yet one step further and recognize the benefits of her strengths to your team and the greater organization.

- Your recognition may be most powerful when offered in a public forum. Yet sometimes that will activate in others excessive envy and competition. Also bear in mind that your appreciation might be "too much" to hear depending on the recipient's culture and personality. So, in all cases, calibrate your appreciation depending on the needs of the particular person and situation.

ACTIONS TO ENHANCE YOUR POWER

- Now that you know how to give people the deepest forms of recognition, conduct an experiment. Each day, provide sincere validation to at least one individual who works for you. At a minimum, use the tools of first order appreciation. But try the second order techniques too. Then closely observe the impact on each person. See if it's not motivating him or her to make greater contributions. Next, take your appreciation practice into your relationships with your spouse, other family members, and friends. As you give your validation so generously, notice what comes back in return.

GALVANIZE OTHERS WITH DEEPLY SHARED VALUES, A COMMON MISSION, AND YOUR CONVICTION

Extend the power of your inspiration by establishing a set of values and a mission for those you are leading. Ensure that the values are profound commitments made by you and your people about how you will act with each other. Let these values emerge from your group and then give a voice to them and confirm them in writing. Heighten the inspiration of your people further with a compelling mission that stirs them. Let it be something they can envision and that will make a significant contribution. And show your bold conviction that you, as a group, will achieve it. When you have such faith in your collective power, your people will have faith, too. And then that power will all the more likely come to fruition.

To more deeply inspire those you lead, unite them around a set of values and a mission that speaks to them and that moves them. Such collective meaning and purpose binds people together and guides them. We talked about establishing values and a mission for yourself in Chapter 7. When you also do this for others, you are a more inspirational and more powerful leader.

Values are the fundamental guidelines that people work by and live by. If you lead a sizable organization or some other large group of people, state the common values for them. Of course, respect the limits of your leadership and only state values related to your common endeavor. And even then, do not simply impose them. If you do, the values will become mere rules that others resist—or obey without inspiration. So instead, read the sentiments of the group members and reflect back the important values that you discern. Let the values be a collective truth that you speak for them.

With a smaller group or your own team, guide the members in choosing their values jointly. Ensure that they participate fully and steer them toward unanimous agreement and buy-in. Then they will more "own" the values and be more committed to them. So bring your team together and ask, "What behaviors will we expect of each other? What are the commitments we wish to make to one another?" Then guide them in choosing at least three answers, but no more than ten. Having more values than that risks diluting all of them.

To make your team's values most powerful, frame them in the form of "We will" statements. Then, instead of a generic list of items such as "honesty" and "hard work," you and your team will have a more compelling set of mutual commitments. For example, a team value may be, "We will 100 percent support each other's dignity and efforts." Or, "We will not let down our clients." You can make your team values even more inspirational by adding the words "always" or "never." For example, "We will *always* be there for each other."

Once you have agreed to your team values, put them in writing. And then display them in places where you and your team members will continuously see them and be reminded of them. But merely posting your values does not provide them adequate protection. People will naturally test them, and in fact, it is a common human need to do so. They'll want to see that the values are truly binding commitments rather than just some words that initially felt good to write on a board or a piece of paper.

So make an agreement among the team members that each will speak up upon observing a values infraction. And ensure all the members understand not only that they are permitted to do so, but also that it is an expectation. Boldly state that you, too, want to be told when you violate any of your team's values. In this way, all the team members are empowered to protect this key element of their own inspiration. By using and honoring this approach, you will collectively provide your values a solid protection.

To be truly inspirational, also unite your team and your organization with a common mission. Your people need a clear sense of their collective goals and objectives. And you as their leader are the person to provide that to them. Although values are best determined together, the single-pointed thrust of the mission necessarily comes from the leader.

Let the mission envision something that your people can imagine and actually see. And let it be something that deeply stirs them on an emotional level. If the mission is only to make more money, that may not be most moving for them. So see if you can also make your mission about some greater contribution. See if you can make it about something that will deepen the shared meaning of your mutual efforts. When your mission is more about people, it will be more inspirational. Inspiration, after all, is about the spirit that unites all individuals.

Once you have defined the mission, ensure that your people know it. Ensure, also, that they use it in choosing what to do and what not to do. And ensure that they are always driving toward it. Let the mission be a beacon for them. Let it be a brilliant light toward which they relentlessly move, all together, even in times of great darkness and confusion.

And then, to deepen your power of inspiration even further, state with conviction that you will indeed accomplish your mission. Make a choice to boldly believe in yourself and in your people—and what you can all accomplish together. When your colleagues observe your ardent belief in what will happen, they will believe in it, too. People need something to believe in, especially if they are to be inspired. When you provide that to them, you are more inspirational and more powerful.

You may see obstacles in front of you and yet more obstacles on the horizon. You may see countless reasons why your mission may not be successful. But ask yourself, "What makes me more powerful—pessimism or optimism?" And ask, "What is more likely to move and energize and inspire my people?" Then act, and even think, accordingly. The more you constellate impassioned belief in your ultimate and shared success, the more likely it will happen.

You may be tempted to hedge and not commit yourself fully. But try to avoid waffling and being equivocal. When Dr. Martin Luther King gave his last and deeply inspired speech, he did not say, "Barring unforeseen factors, we will likely get to the promised land." He did not even say, "I hope we'll get to the promised land." Rather, he simply declared, "We, as a people, *will* get to the promised land." Try being that committed and that powerful, too. Then watch and see how people respond.

So consider being a truly inspirational force for those you lead. Declare for them your common values and purpose. Inspire them in your utter commitment to your collective mission. By so claiming all your power, you will make your team, your organization, and your people so much more powerful, too.

KEY POINTS TO REMEMBER

- Unite those you lead by guiding them in adopting a set of inspiring values. These values will be your team members' commitments to one another about how they will show up for each other. Of course, it is important that you commit to these values, too.

- The team values will almost certainly be tested, as it is human nature to do so. Accordingly, protect them by empowering every member of your team to speak up when they observe their violation.

- Further unite and inspire your team by declaring a distinct and powerful mission that moves them. Let the mission envision a tangible and exciting result. And let it be about making a major contribution.

- State with absolute conviction that you will indeed accomplish your mission. Choose to boldly believe in yourself and in your people. Your belief and your commitment will inspire them to believe and commit, too. And that will render you—and them—more powerful.

ACTIONS TO ENHANCE YOUR POWER

- If you lead a team, convene it to establish your collective values. Your team may already have a generic list of values, but unless the members actually crafted them and are all fully committed to them, consider replacing them with the results of this exercise. With all your people together in the same room, ask them, "What are the commitments we want to make to one another in how we'll act and show up for each other?" Ensure that the answers are phrased in terms of "We will" statements as in, "We will always support each other in the pursuit of our mission." You may suggest some values of your own, but ensure that a number of them also come from your team members. And adopt only those values that everyone agrees to. As a result of this process, each team member will likely feel ownership of the values that emerge and will be committed to them.

EPILOGUE

You thought this book was about power. Yet, it's also about love. And to make things happen in your life and in the world, they really must go together. So give your love more generously—to yourself and to others. Then observe the power that awakens within you and beyond you, too.

In the last section of the last chapter, I talked about Martin Luther King's mission. I have a mission, too. It is to provide insight and understanding that transforms negative emotions into positive ones. It transforms darkness into light. Ultimately, it transforms fear and hate into freedom and love. And with this transformation, we can heal the world.

Will you join with me? Will you join with me in bringing more self-awareness into the world? And more compassion? And less fear, anger, and false shame? So much unnecessary suffering happens every day because of these things. And you and I can make a difference. We really can. You do your part and I'll do mine. Let us see what we can make happen together.

Your contribution is needed now. Look around you. Look and see what is happening in our world. Look at all the suffering and torment people cause themselves and each other. Now is the time for you to emerge into the fullness of your power. Great leaders don't arise in times of calm and plenty. They emerge in times of great difficulty and great challenge. In dark times, you can be the bright light that people are drawn to.

So create a vision of the person and the leader you want to be. Envision a state where you have united and integrated the potent energies coursing through you. Envision that magnificent power flowing with such grace and ease that the world cannot help but respond and receive your gifts.

Did you ever think you could be such a leader? You can be, regardless of whether your roles are very expansive or seemingly quite ordinary. It's enough for you to focus on your regular interactions in your everyday life. Stay self-aware. Don't let anger, fear, and false shame govern your actions. Have compassion. Hold your dignity. Hold your power. When you act in these ways, you show people a different way of being. And they will learn from you. And then they will teach others in the same way. Your impact will ripple outward—really, across the planet. It will happen imperceptibly, yet powerfully. You are far more powerful than you realize.

Join with me. Let us see what we can make happen together.

INDEX

self-awareness
  awareness of how one loses
    oneself, 174–78
  expanding, 24–32
  gaps in, 26
  impact on results, 25f
  managing emotions and, 188–89
  See also self-possession
self-betrayal, 46–47
  awareness of how one loses
    oneself, 174–78
  defined, 175
  transforming it into integrity,
    176–78, 189, 193, 196
  See also Five Gifts Roadmap
self-disclosure, 160
self-doubt, 38, 45
  actions to disprove, 107–10
  See also false shame; Five Gifts
    Roadmap
self-possession
  defined, 120, 121
  transforming anger by, 120–25
self-rejection of false shame,
    countered with self-
    acceptance, 97–100
shame
  defined, 85
  See also false shame
shame-based competition, 89
speaking openly and authentically,
    158–64
spirit, 16–17, 240–41. *See also*
  inspiration

spontaneity, 69
success, internal
  vs. external success, 193
  prioritizing, 192–96

T
"team spirit," 16
team values, 257–60. *See also* values
transference, 232–34
  defined, 232
triggers of anger, deeper, 123

U
understanding
  defined, 128
  other people, using psychological
    insight for, 231–36
  those who provoke you, 127–31
  See also PEA chain(s)
uniting with other people, 245–48

V
values, 181–83
  defined, 182
  galvanizing others with deeply
    shared, 257–60
  solidifying your commitments to
    your, 180–85

W
"We will" statements, 258

ACKNOWLEDGMENTS

I wish to thank all the clients with whom I have had the honor of working over the years. Their courage, exploration, and commitment enabled much of my own growth as a psychologist, a consultant, and a human being. I feel honored to have worked with so many extraordinary individuals.

I am also greatly indebted to the many teachers who have guided me and instructed me along the way. I have had far too many to list here. My hope is to pass on their wisdom to others with as much generosity and kindness as they showed me.

Many people offered their thoughtful suggestions as I was developing the manuscript. I am grateful to them all. Four were especially generous in all the efforts they made on my behalf. My sincere thanks to Dave Barton, Catherine Crusade, Adam Koren, and Victoria Mausisa. Your contributions were a great aid in my writing of this book. I also want to thank Ann Demarais, whose wise counsel, although difficult to hear at times, has been very valuable to me. Special thanks to Lisa Vega, whose friendship and advice were so precious in the very difficult early stages of this project.

And finally, in deep gratitude, I thank Russell Wikander, who passed before this book was completed—and who offered me heartfelt and abundant support without which the book may not have been possible. I am forever touched by his immense generosity and kindness of spirit.

ABOUT THE AUTHOR

Dean Herman, Ph.D., is a psychologist and executive consultant. He has worked with thousands of executives and business leaders in North America, Europe, Asia, and Australia to enhance their performance. Organizations Dean has assisted include Hewlett-Packard, Toyota, Siemens, Wells Fargo, Agilent Technologies, Sun Microsystems/Oracle, Bertelsmann, LG Life Sciences/LG Electronics, Nestlé, Texas Instruments, and McKinsey & Company.

As a holder of a Ph.D. in clinical psychology, Dean brings the wisdom and power of psychology to organizational leaders in ways that are accessible and transformative. Dean is based in San Francisco and you can reach him at www.hermanconsulting.com and www.fourportals .com.

FOR MORE INFORMATION

Dean Herman, Ph.D., consults to individual leaders as well as their teams. He also provides workshops, seminars, and keynote talks on a variety of topics. To learn more about Dean's services, please contact:

Herman Consulting
555 California Street, Suite 300
San Francisco, California 94104
Telephone: 415-296-0220
Dean@hermanconsulting.com
www.hermanconsulting.com

To order an electronic version of this book, go to www.fourportals.com.

To receive Dean Herman's monthly email newsletter, email Dean at info@hermanconsulting.com.